My Little Cowboy

Also by Roger Mendoza:

Non-Fiction:

My Little Cowboy, First Edition

Fiction:

Purging Purgatory: A Ghost Story

The E. B. Roberts Chronicles:
Alexander's Journey (No. 1)
The Sheriff (No. 2)
Broken Widow (No. 3)

My Little Cowboy

My Reincarnation Story

Second Edition

ROGER MENDOZA

Published by: *ROMEN* **Graphics**
www.RomenGraphics.com

Book website: www.MyLittleCowboy.com

No part of this publication may be reproduced, stored in a retrieval system, or transmitted, in any form, or by any means, electronic, mechanical, photocopying, recording, or otherwise, without the prior consent of the author or publisher (except for the inclusion of brief quotations in a review).

The content of this book is solely the opinion and factual life experience of the author. Some people's names used in this book were changed to protect their privacy. All individuals mentioned in this book do not necessarily agree with the views of the author or the premise of this book.

While the author and publisher have used their best efforts in preparing this book, they make no representations or warranties with respect to the accuracy or completeness of the contents of this book.

Cover Photography Roger Mendoza

Copyright © 2012, 2016 by Roger Mendoza

All rights reserved, First edition 2012.
Second edition 2016.

ISBN: Paperback ed.   978-1-938962-20-2
ISBN: Hardcover ed.   978-1-938962-21-9

Library of Congress Control Number: 2016954768

DEDICATION

To my mother - Carmen,
She called me to this life and nurtured and cared for me.

To my friend, who was once called Alex.
He taught me balance, patience and a willingness to live.

To my dog - Einstein,
He taught me how to love unconditionally.

CONTENTS

DEDICATION v
CONTENTS vii
PREFACE TO SECOND EDITION ix
INTRODUCTION 1
1 5
2 9
3 15
4 21
5 25
6 29
7 33
8 39
9 43
10 51
11 55
12 61
13 67
14 75
15 81
16 87
17 91
18 97
19 101
20 107
21 111

22	117
23	123
24	129
25	137
26	143
27	151
28	157
29	163
30	171
ACKNOWLEDGMENTS	177
PRINCIPLES	179
CHRONOLOGY OF EVENTS	181
ABOUT THE AUTHOR	183
BOOK CLUB QUESTIONS	185

PREFACE TO SECOND EDITION

This book is about reincarnation. It is about my past lives, two in particular. Although, I have lived many lives before this one.

Do you believe in reincarnation? I do. After experiencing the past life recall episode that I describe in this book, how could I not?

Do you believe that your soul is separate from your physical body? Do you believe that your soul is the real you? I believe those things and more.

Here is what I think reincarnation is:

I believe all souls were created at once, eons ago. I don't know when and I don't really care to know. I do believe in God and that he created those souls. You might be thinking that I'm a creationist (i.e. a believer that God created man, not evolution). However, that would be incorrect. I believe that evolution is responsible for what we now call man (or woman). I believe that the soul and the physical body are two separate things. The soul is a life force that lives forever. The physical body is born, lives for a while (hopefully) and then dies.

Are you still with me?

Good!

There is a third component, of who we are, though.

Time to get your pitchforks and torches ready.

I call the third component of man (or woman) a thought-collective. It is an aspect of the soul.

A thought-collective is an ever expanding repository of all thoughts uniquely (and permanently) tied to a particular soul. Each and every soul is associated with its own unique thought-collective.

Each person is born with a soul and its associated thought-collective. As the person experiences life (by thinking thoughts), his/her thought-collective expands. Every experience, whether positive or negative is represented in that soul's associated thought-collective. In other words, every thought ever thought by the person is aggregated into his/her soul's thought-collective. This thought-collective forms the beliefs of the living individual. The thought-collective and its associated soul together define the core attitudes and personality of the individual. When the person dies, this thought-collective and its associated soul continue to exist.

Some people believe that the soul is born into one and only one body, never to be born into another body again. I don't.

I believe that each soul (and its associated thought-collective) is unique and can be born into a body that eventually dies and then that same soul can be born into a new body. For most people this cycle is repeated many times. Each cycle (i.e. incarnation) expands the thought-collective.

The thought-collective is the aggregation of all of the thoughts and experiences of the current life and of all of the previous lives lived by a unique soul.

Heresy, you say!

This 'soul-mind-body' concept makes sense to me. For a living person: The soul is the life force expressed through emotion; The thought-collective is expressed through the mind; The body is the core attitudes and personality expressed through health.

The soul and its associated thought-collective never cease to exist.

Please put your pitchforks and torches away as I continue.

Years ago, before I ever wrote this book, I made a wish; perhaps it was a prayer.

"Please let me understand why I am the way I am."

I asked because I was tired of living a life where I felt that this world would be better off without me. Yes. I thought about killing myself a few times. I finally tried it and failed. I ended up in the hospital and was much better for it. I learned how to dance and to better express myself. Fortunately, I didn't lose my job – a software engineer in the defense industry.

Even though I was much better off than before. I still felt a longing to find someone that was missing from my life. It wasn't like the way people described looking for their soul mate. It was something different. It felt like finding a person who had once meant so much to me and then lost. Well, in this life, I never lost any such person, and I had no reason to miss anyone. And, to be honest, I preferred to not be in a relationship with somebody. I'm a loner, and I like that very much.

In, 1980 I saw the movie "Somewhere in Time" and it resonated with me. Christopher Reeve's character (Richard Collier) "remembers" Jane Seymour's character (Elise McKenna) after seeing a picture of her. Richard Collier "remembered" his relationship with Elise. Although, the relationship happened years before he was even born. I love that movie. It is my all-time favorite. That movie resonated with me. Even though it is about time travel. I thought of it as a story about reincarnation.

Just a couple of years later, I met someone that resonated with me similarly, to how Elise McKenna did to Richard Collier in the movie "Somewhere in Time." It bothered me and sometimes angered me that something was happening to me that I didn't understand. How could I remember a person who I had never met before? This can only occur in the movies, I thought.

Well, several years passed, during which my life was filled with wanting to solve this painful riddle: Why do I want this person, this stranger in my life? Especially now that he thinks I am nuts.

Mind you, I still wanted to end my life. I'd been obsessing over this person for over twenty years.

Then, in 2005 the "hallucination" happened on my way to work. I saw him, the object of my obsession in the 1800's. Suddenly my desire to end my life was lessened, and I had a new obsession. Why did I have such a "hallucinogenic" experience? Now, I had daily intrusions of this "hallucination."

No, I wasn't taking drugs!

These intrusions were so distracting from my obsession with this person that I started to get excited about life again.

Then in 2008, I had a life threatening issue that almost killed me – a bleeding ulcer where I lost more than half of my blood. During that episode, I fought hard to stay alive, even though it would have been easier to just let myself die. I ended up in the hospital. When I was released, I was better than new. I realized that I didn't want to die anymore.

Once I wrote this book, the hallucinogenic intrusions disappeared from my life. Later, I moved back to my hometown of San Antonio and found that I had a renewed sense of self. I learned that the experiences of the past were best left in the past. All of the good and bad experiences of the past were what made me what I am today.

I believe that my past includes not only this life but also all of the lives I (my soul and its associated collection of thoughts) have lived before.

As for the person with whom I was obsessed with? He's happily married with four children (at last count) and moved on with his life. Most people do not (and should not) remember their past lives. In retrospect, I'm thankful that he didn't remember his past life. That would have been awkward.

I used to think that dreams never come true for me until I wished that I could remember my past lives. My wish came true, and now I remember more than anyone should. I didn't realize that past lives are meant to grow from – not to relive.

My takeaway: Live in the present, not the past and not the future. Appreciate the relationships in your life and cherish the respect that others have for you. And most of all, cherish the respect you have for yourself.

And, have respect for your soul, your body, and your mind. They are a great combination that makes you who you are.

This is a story about how life stories always have happy endings (no matter how tragic the journey). This is a story about how each life always coalesces into an incredible, contrast filled, universe-expanding life.

This is a story about how people's lives always continue in spite of interruptions. Life always finds a way to bliss, if you let it.

INTRODUCTION

One morning in May 2005 as I was driving on my seventeen-mile trek to work, I decided to put a meditation CD into my player. The cover of the CD had a warning advising that you should not drive while listening to the meditation. I blatantly ignored the warning and pushed play. The road was not well traveled. I could quickly hit the stop button if I needed to. I couldn't see any problems with doing this. I found it to have beautiful and soothing music with nice calming words. My mind began to wander and imagery from different historical periods began to flood my thoughts. I thought about the wagon wheels, the highway road, the horses, the steering wheel, the covered wagons, the highway signs, and my car on the road traveling on the road.

Barely fifteen minutes into the CD, I felt a level of clarity that I had never experienced before. I became super aware of my driving and the wheels of a stagecoach all at the same time. I could see a version of myself meeting a woman, marry, raise children, and much more. The freeway exit caught my attention. It jolted me back to the subject of my work, my car, and the highway. As quickly as I had shifted into an expanded focus of hyper-awareness, my focus had shifted to an awareness of my job. My job was not very pleasant, so just the thought of going into work was not much different than slapping me across my face. I realized that what I had just experienced had characteristics similar to a waking dream. There was so much information in it. It had the qualities of a holographic image where you could see an infinite number of perspectives. If I focused on the wagon, I could discern the minutest of details about the wagon. It seemed that I could look at any aspect of the scene and know many intimate details. If I focused on the other version of myself in the dream, I knew all about that man. When I focused on the woman, I could see that she was my wife in the dream, what she looked like, how she moved, and even her mannerisms. It was quite odd. No matter where I focused, I knew all about the story – this story.

When I got to work, I scribbled some notes and then tried to focus on my job. When I got home, I wrote down as much detail as I could remember. As I fell asleep that night, I wondered if I had dreamt about my past life. There was so much information. I wanted to know more. I wanted to know what happened next since the story had seemed to end abruptly. I had a feeling that the story had a tragic ending, but I wasn't sure. I had plenty to think about as I drifted off to sleep.

A couple of months later (July 2005), I was taking a road trip to San Antonio with my brother's family. I had just completed six hours of driving and pulled over for a short break. It was my brother's turn to drive, so I went over to the passenger side and made myself comfortable as my brother took over the task of driving. I started to doze off, and what seemed to be an instant later I was in a waking dream. I saw the second half of the story unfold in the same holographic manner as the first half had done two months earlier. However, this time, I saw the tragic ending. It was unsettling, to say the least. I woke up with a start and told my brother. I could tell that he was less than impressed. He was in his rhythmic driving pattern, probably thinking about his life questions (mostly finance, I'm sure). I probably startled him, and he figured I was making a big deal about a silly dream. I don't blame him. Nevertheless, to me, it was a phenomenal, multidimensional holographic dream.

When we arrived in San Antonio, I documented my experience. Once I committed these happenings to paper, then the wagon wheels and horses that seemed to dominate my imaginings had vanished. This blew me away. Could this be for real? It was as if these imaginings had been trying to get my attention for years. I began to see connections in that story to this life. At times, the connections seemed to have far-reaching implications that were impossible for me to ignore. The son from that story in the 1800's is the same person as a close friend from whom I've been estranged for the last thirty years. I even recognized myself as the father. That life and this life - my life were inexplicably intertwined.

What follows is a narrative of that story that I once lived. It was the life that has profoundly affected this life.

1

It was late September of 1864. The air was crisp and fresh. The birds flew from tree to tree announcing the new day. Their cacophony of singing was almost deafening. The trees nearest to the two story hotel held hundreds of squawking crows. They carefully watched the suspicious man below from their perch.

Alexander, a tall, thin man in his late forties was almost alone in the town square waiting for the stagecoach as he paced back and forth in the middle of the reddish brown hard clay road. He looked like a banker or a businessman with his fine woolen tan pants and his well shined dark boots. He pulled out his gold pocket watch while he was still pacing on the dusty road. He knew that the stagecoach would have to stop at the bank to load some valuable cargo before picking him up in front of his hotel. The coach should have already arrived, he thought. He would have been worried about the cargo, but he had the assurance from the town sheriff that all would go well. It was already seven in the morning. He took a deep breath and let it out all at once. He would just have to wait. He hated waiting with a passion.

Alexander was a very solitary man. Always friendly, well liked and proficient at everything that he did. He worked as a bank manager, usually staying in the big city. He rarely traveled to the smaller banks in the towns nearby. Instead, he would conduct most of his bank business between his hometown of San Francisco, a thriving gold rush town and the major banks of New York. However, two days before he had traveled to this small town about a day's ride from his home to visit with his eldest son under the guise of conducting bank business. He was very familiar with this town but never had much interest in visiting. He was much more comfortable with the feel of the big city. Even San Francisco was no comparison to New York City, the city where he had grown up. He had traveled with his wife and infant son from New York to San Francisco long ago.

What could anyone, even his son find comfortable about this small town in the middle of nowhere? He took a deep breath and let it out all at once. "Where is that damn coach?" Alexander said.

Alexander had lost his wife, the love of his life some thirteen years back. He never wanted to get married again. How could he even think about it? He had two sons and a daughter. His oldest, Alex was twenty-three then Marcus nineteen and Marissa sixteen. He loved his children and was very proud of each.

The waiting was unbearable. Still no coach. Alexander made his way to the hotel porch as horses, carts, and people began their hustle and bustle along the roadway. He kept to himself and didn't make eye contact with any of the townspeople. Most people didn't pay attention to this stranger. They just went about their business, not quite sure what to make of him. However, some of the townspeople glared at him as he nervously paced back and forth. They weren't sure what he was up to. Probably up to no good, they thought. Even the crows watched him silently, occasionally squawking with suspicion.

Alexander was lost in thought, impatient and distracted. He didn't notice that it was a beautiful cloudless blue sky. There were two dogs in the alley next door to the saloon where he had met the sheriff when he first came to town. He didn't hear the rhythmical sound of the horses' hoofs as they passed by him. Up the street from the hotel, he saw the town grocer, a shoe repair store, a blacksmith shop, and the town jail. The town was coming to life.

At half past eight, beautiful majestic horses pulling a shiny black stagecoach arrived in front of the hotel. Alexander snapped out of his distraction in time to see the driver motioning him to enter the coach. He took one last look up and down the street and hesitated before entering the stagecoach. Was this all for naught, he wondered. His heart was crushed. There were two other passengers already seated in the coach. They were a wealthy couple named Charles and Victoria Adams. Alexander was familiar with them, as they were loyal bank customers who frequented the bank where he worked. Alexander was not shy. He graciously participated in the obligatory pleasantries of exchanging greetings with his traveling companions.

Victoria noticed that Alexander looked a bit pale and asked, "You don't look very well, Mr. Johnson. Are you alright?"

He was devastated. He had been sure that his son was coming back home with him. I told him that it was his choice. His son had seemed thrilled at the prospect of seeing his siblings and Gertrude again.

"I'm just tired from all of this bank business. If you don't mind, I'll close my eyes for a bit and see if I can get a bit of rest."

Alexander leaned up against the side of the coach, pulled his hat over his face and shut his eyes. He felt defeated and just wanted to go home. With that, the coach drove on.

Alexander quickly fell asleep and found himself dreaming of his father. In the dream, Alexander's father was furious with him. His father was very abusive, self-centered, and drank excessively. His father was yelling at Alexander. His father was telling Alexander that he was worthless. In his dream, Alexander was only twelve years old. Alexander thought that if he couldn't get his father's love, then he would at least try to get his father's respect. His father thought that this was ridiculous. His father was laughing at him, ridiculing him, and taunting him. Alexander woke up agitated and choking.

This time, Charles asked, "Are you alright? You seem distressed."

Alexander, using his might to gather his composure, sat upright. "Yes, I'm fine. I just had a bad dream. I apologize for upsetting your wife."

Victoria smiled uncomfortably.

Charles continued, "Alexander, do you know what business this coach had with the bank this morning? I saw them loading some satchels into the compartment above."

Alexander took a deep breath and let it out all at once.

"Just a small sum of money to transfer back to the central bank branch. There is nothing to worry about."

Victoria shifted uneasily in her seat with a look of sheer panic on her face. Even before she could gasp, she knew instantly that something was terribly wrong. She had a sense for these sorts of things. The stagecoach was traveling on a narrow road when a shot was fired, instantly killing the driver. The horses ran in terror. Victoria, Charles, and Alexander were jostled about in the cabin as the coach careened over the edge of the trail into the ravine. Alexander was thrown out of the coach seconds before the it stopped at the bottom. Alexander saw someone up on the road above. He wiped away at the blood that was obscuring his vision.

"I'll get some help," he muttered. Alexander crawled up the side of the ravine. As he crawled onto the road, he saw his son's friend Tom seated on his horse.

"We've had an accident, we need help. My travel companions are still alive down there, but the driver is dead," Alexander cried.

Tom got down from his horse to help Alexander.

Alexander could still hear Victoria sobbing quietly. Alexander jumped as he heard Victoria scream. Two loud shots silenced her scream. Even the birds went silent.

Alexander laid still on the ground, writhing in pain fading in and out of consciousness. He thought that he was dreaming again. The pain in his left leg was intense. It was broken. With a mixture of tears and blood in his eyes, he looked up at Tom and said, "Help!" Then Alexander passed out and began to dream about his wife, Martha.

2

Martha had long and thick dark almost-black hair. It fell straight down a couple of inches passed her shoulder. She had large, warm dark brown eyes. Martha was a very independent, self-sufficient woman. This was unusual for a woman in 1838 New York. Only seventeen years old, she had already planned the rest of her life. Martha planned to complete college, get a serious job, and then marry. Her father, whom she loved with all of her heart, was not so keen about her determination to pursue a college degree. He would often tell Martha that most women were quite happy to just marry and have children. Martha was his only child, and he wanted everything for her. She was quite ambitious for a woman of her day. She didn't care, though. She was determined to do things her way, no matter what.

Growing up, Martha excelled in her early school studies. She was very competitive and outperformed every boy in arithmetic and reading. She loved reading and found that she had a natural knack for arithmetic. She felt compelled to spend her free time reading one of the many books that she would carefully sneak out of her father's library. She was always careful to return the book back to its rightful place in the library. Her father was so proud of his daughter. He always knew when a book was missing and found it amusing that his daughter thought that it would bother him that she borrowed a book. He often told his wife how proud he was of their daughter. Martha's mother was content to run the household and manage all of the important household matters, except for the finances. Her favorite pastime was knitting. She had hoped that her only child would spend more time learning how to be a proper young woman. She knew that times were changing, and perhaps it was not such a bad thing that Martha was developing a strong independent nature. She loved that quality so much in her husband. And, of course, she loved her daughter with all of her heart.

Martha left home to start college. It was exciting for her. She was on her own, and she loved it. She was just about to start her second year of college when Gertrude, a close companion of Martha's mother, sent word that Martha's parents were in a fatal stagecoach accident. She didn't know that her parents were actually killed by stagecoach robbers looking for money and jewels. The thieves had known that her parents were very wealthy. Martha left school and returned to her parent's home to tend to their funeral. After her tragic loss, she lost interest in returning to college. Perhaps later, she thought. She knew that as a woman, she would not be able to maintain the lifestyle to which she was accustomed. That is when she decided to use what she did learn in college to obtain employment. She found work very quickly with the local town bank. Martha learned that life takes good care of you if you let it.

In spite of her very independent outlook on life, she was the most kind-hearted and generous person in the bank. All of her co-workers loved her and thought very highly of her. She always completed her work ahead of schedule and was never tardy for work. After a few weeks of work, she noticed that one of the bank managers was throwing glances her way several times throughout the day. This made her feel very uncomfortable. She had no interest in men. She was there simply to save enough money to return to school even though her inheritance would have allowed her to live a comfortable life. She wanted much more. One day, he was waiting for her just outside of the building. He'd been waiting a few minutes already and had turned to walk back into the building. She must have gone out through the back entrance, he thought. He stepped forward and nearly collided with Martha.

"Excuse me!" he said.

"What? Why are you stalking me like a common criminal? I didn't see you there," she was startled, and her words seemed to take on a life of their own. Her temper was flaring. "I've noticed you gazing at me while I'm trying to do my job. You must know that this is highly improper," she condescended.

She looked at his face and then his eyes. They went from their usual bright boyish charm to wide-eyed darkness and confusion. She hurt him, and she regretted it. Even so, she was a proper woman.

"I'm so sorry! I just wanted to ask you if you would do me the honor of accompanying me to the church picnic this Sunday. I thought it would be an excellent opportunity for us to get to know each other." He presented a cool, calm demeanor with just the right amount of suave.

"Well! You certainly are forward; I'll give you that. Now, why would I want to go with you? You know nothing about me, and I don't know anything about you," she said.

She was both annoyed and intrigued all at the same time. Alexander was an attractive young man that reminded her very much of her father. She liked that he was always courteous and considerate to her. Even so, she was torn between her plans for her future, which didn't include men until she was finished with her college, and her heart. She was still mourning the loss of her parents. She had decided that living in her parent's home in New York would give her time to gain some experience in banking. After a year or two, she would return to school. She had already completed one year and planned to complete her studies in business. Martha remained unconvinced that this was a man's world.

Alexander smiled.

"That is precisely why I've asked you to the picnic. What better way to get to know each other while in the midst of our 'God-fearing' neighbors."

Alexander stayed the course.

"And why would we need to know each other any more than we already do. When I complete my assignments, Mr. Johnson, don't I deliver them to you in a professional manner?"

"Of course you do, Martha. Please call me by my given name. It is Alexander," he said, his smile fading.

Now, he was getting annoyed. All of the other bank employees called him by his first name, except for Martha. Alexander was not a very patient man, even though he was used to dealing with difficult customers almost every day. He managed to subdue this shortcoming when dealing with them. She was different than they were. Martha was not a difficult woman, but rather a strong woman. This was something that Alexander truly admired about her. He breathed in slowly and let it out just as slowly. He felt less annoyed.

"Alexander-" she started.

"Or you can call me Alex," he interrupted.

"Mr. Johnson! I mean Alexander! Please, do not presume to..."

"I'm sorry. Alexander would be perfect," said Alexander, his smile returning.

"And you may call me Martha. Now, what time did you say that picnic starts?"

"I didn't. It starts about 10:00. May I call on you at 10:30?"

"No, you may not. I would prefer that you call on me at 11:00 sharp. My sister and I will be ready by then," she said as she looked away, hoping that he would not notice that she would enjoy his company more if she had someone to talk to during the picnic (other than him). At least, that is what she told herself. It was a lie. He had caught her attention on her second day on the job. She felt a strange feeling of recognition that she had never felt before. She thought that maybe she had met him at the train station when she returned from school. Or, perhaps she'd met him at the University. It really didn't matter, she thought. She met many people along the way and soon forgot most of them. Mr. Alexander Johnson was different, she couldn't just forget him, she worked with him every day.

"Your sister?" he said. He thought that Martha had no siblings. Perhaps he had misunderstood her when she hired onto the bank. "Oh yes, of course. I will pick you up promptly at 11:00. Please don't be late."

He knew that she was always prompt because he usually arrived at least an hour or more before she did. She always arrived at the bank precisely ten minutes before the bank opened.

"Good day, Martha. I look forward to seeing you and your sister on Sunday."

"Good day to you, Mr. Johnson," she said as she turned away with a smirk on her face. She had a pronounced lightness in her step, as she seemed to glide away like a beautiful swan.

"Mr. Johnson?" he muttered to himself. "It's Alexander."

She heard him, and her smirk changed to a broad smile. "I must tell Gertrude the fantastic news," she whispered. She always told Gertrude everything.

3

Alexander had often dreamt of meeting just such a woman. She not only looked familiar to him but felt familiar too. Nonsense, he thought to himself. He could not understand how he could dream about a woman that he had never met. It is just a coincidence. It was an incredible coincidence, he reassured himself. Even so, he had on occasion dreamt about things that had not yet happened.

As a young boy, he had once made the mistake of assuming that everyone had these sorts of dreams. He told his schoolmates about one of his dreams where the beloved schoolmaster died during a horse-riding incident. All of the children made fun of Alexander. When the schoolmaster heard of the tale, he promptly punished Alexander for spreading such nonsense. The schoolmaster spoke with Alexander's father later that evening. After the schoolmaster had left, Alexander's father beat him severely. The next day the schoolmaster died. He'd fallen from his horse, just as Alexander had dreamt. Alexander was only ten years old, and living alone with his father. Alexander had arrived at school that day, still sore from the beating he'd received. He mourned the loss of his beloved schoolmaster alone. The other children distanced themselves from him, calling him strange.

Alexander brushed away the thought of this painful memory. There were many of these sorts of memories concerning his father, but this one was the worst one of them all. Father was a good-for-nothing drunk, he thought.

Alexander's awareness snapped back just in time to see Martha several yards away as she briskly slipped around the corner. What a beautiful woman, he thought. He felt triumphant that his plan had worked. He had exited the building quietly through the back door and had come around the front to catch Martha as she was leaving work. He'd been planning this for several days, even though he was very nervous about it. He had felt like an adolescent boy working up the courage to ask a girl to a church dance. He was thrilled that she had accepted his invitation to the picnic. Here was a smart, pretty and a very independent woman who stirred his heart in a way that felt both familiar and foreign to him at the same time. Memories of his mother started to play out in his mind, just long enough for him to brush them away. No! He would not go there.

Alexander looked back at the bank and decided that he should get back to work. It had already been a long day, but he had work to finish. He went back into the building and made his way to his desk. The bank was nearly empty. His office was located away from the counters where the customer transactions occurred. It was down a narrow corridor that was near to a modest grouping of four desks (one of them was where Martha usually sat). His office was in the far corner with a glass panel inset in a wooden door, through which he could see all of the desks in the larger outer room. His desk was situated in a spacious office that was filled neatly with carefully placed stacks of receipts, invoices, and other important papers. He enjoyed his job and took great pride in his work. The bank owner also had an office next to Alexander's office but rarely used it. The bank owner relied on Alexander and another manager to handle most of the day-to-day bank business. Alexander sat down in his chair and started to look at the bank statement he had been working on before his mad rush to intercept Martha. He looked up and saw Martha's desk through the glass of his door, which held his name MR. ALEXANDER JOHNSON, BANK MANAGER. A modest looking shawl was draped over the back of Martha's chair. He remembered that his mother had always kept a shawl just like it draped over the armrest of her favorite rocker for when she was a little chilly.

Alexander loved his mother. He liked how she would dote on him. He was admittedly spoiled. He was, after all, an only child. He couldn't remember for sure, but he thought that he was about eight or so years old when she died. He didn't know what she had died from. No matter, he thought it was a very long time ago, and he was grateful that he could remember how happy he had been when they would picnic together. The three of them would often go to picnics: he, his mother, and his father. Those were wonderful times, he thought as a smile started to show through his tightly clenched teeth. After his mother had died, his father changed. He went from a man that would occasionally drink to one who would drink himself into a drunken stupor until one day he drank himself to death. He hated what his father had become - a mean drunk who blamed the world for his own misfortune. Alexander paused for a moment and supposed that maybe his father had become unraveled when his wife had died. Odd, Alexander thought, why that hadn't occurred to him before.

Alexander gathered some papers and placed them carefully into his satchel. The sun had not yet settled down for the night, and he wanted to get home. He bade farewell to the other bank manager and rode his horse home.

Alexander remembered the day that his aunt had come to visit him after his father had died. His aunt had brought with her several large crates. Some were so heavy that his aunt had left them on the carriage. He remembered the exchange clearly:

> "Your mother had asked me to keep these things for you until you were older. Now that your father is gone, I thought that you should have them. Could you help the driver with the last two items?" his aunt said excitedly.
>
> Alexander and the coach driver brought the precious cargo into the front room of the house. She opened one of the large trunks and withdrew a small case.
>
> "She asked me to give you this with the rest of your

inheritance. She was hoping that you would use it to go to college," she said as she handed Alexander the case.

The case contained bank notes, several gold coins and a letter carefully placed in an envelope. As he opened it, he noticed a delicate fragrance that reminded him of his mother. He looked over at his aunt then unfolded the letter and started to read.

"My dearest son, I love you very much. I wanted to be sure that you wouldn't have to worry about your future. I'm sure that my sister has told you as much …"

When Alexander finished the last page, his mouth started to quiver. He carefully placed the folded letter back into the envelope and noticed that his aunt was looking at him intently. She leaned forward and hugged him.

"She would tell me often how much she loved you," she said still hugging him.

"Thank you," said Alexander. "Even though I was very young when she passed away, I still remember her."

The memory of the day his aunt had visited him had started to fade as he wiped an errant tear from his cheek. A warm feeling gently caressed him as he remembered what his mother had written to him in that letter. He still had the letter safely tucked away in the top drawer of his desk at home.

Alexander lived relatively close to the bank in the house where he had grown up. It was a modest home. The house was on quite a large property not far from the big city.

As he came up the trail, he saw the large eight-foot wide hitching post just to the right of the front porch. Off to the left was an area that held a large overgrown garden full of weeds and brush. Behind the garden was a large barn that had the same dark, weathered wood as the main house. Both could have used some paint.

Alexander walked up the wooden steps to the large wide porch that stretched the full width of the house. He'd always thought it was odd that the steps were not in the middle of the porch like most houses, but rather on the side closest to the hitching post. The front door was in the middle of the porch, with a comfortable, creaky swing chair along the far side of the porch. The swing was almost as wide as the porch was deep, about six feet.

Alexander walked into his house and prepared his supper. He enjoyed cooking. Every now and then, his neighbor, a longtime friend of his mother, would leave something for him. Alexander didn't spend much time visiting his neighbors. He didn't have much time for anything but chores when he got home. Even so, he definitely appreciated his mother's friend. They never really talked much, except to thank her with a few dollars now and again. Once, she had started to tell him about his mother. He would interrupt her and then politely asked her to refrain from doing that. She had noticed that his eyes had begun to well up, and she promised never discussed his mother with him again.

After supper, Alexander fed his horse and then spent the next couple of hours completing his chores. There was so much work to do around his house. He sometimes thought that he should buy a smaller place in the city and forgo the maintenance that was required for such a large property. He rationalized that he made a very nice salary as a bank manager, and he could afford to hire a hand to better care for his property if he really wanted to stay there. No matter, he thought. He made his way back to the house, cleaned up and retired for the day. He had finished his chores much quicker than usual. He still felt energetic and happy, a feeling he hadn't felt since before his mother died. He thought about Martha as he drifted off to sleep.

4

Martha wasted no time in telling Gertrude every detail about Alexander.

"He is the most wonderful man that I have ever met," said Martha. The words were flying out of her mouth with hardly a breath of air between her words.

"I've noticed for weeks now that he's been interested in me. I thought it was hardly proper to..." Martha hadn't noticed that Gertrude had started to drift off in thought.

A memory flittered through Gertrude's heart that reverberated throughout her entire being. She remembered her beloved childhood sweetheart. She was a young woman of fifteen years when she met John. He was the most handsome and smartest man that she had ever known. After three years of courtship, John and Gertrude decided to marry.

John was the only sibling of Martha's Mother. He was twenty-one years old, and his sister, Mary (Martha's mother) had turned twenty-four years old on John and Gertrude's wedding day. Gertrude was extroverted, and John was very introverted. What a great combination, Gertrude thought. Gertrude had waited patiently for John to propose. Gertrude was a very patient woman, in spite of her natural extroverted nature. She relished the anticipation and excitement of how things unfolded. She dreamed of spending the rest of her life with him.

It was a beautiful spring day on the day of her wedding. She was dressed in the prettiest billowy, lacey dress. Everything was perfect, she thought. However, the marriage was not to be. Gertrude found that her beloved John had been fatally injured on the morning of her wedding.

John had gotten up early that day, and rode his prized horse. Through a freak accident, he'd fallen from his horse and was knocked unconscious. He was bleeding severely when he was found. His family sent word to Gertrude to come. She rushed to his bedside and arrived just in time for John to utter, "I love you."

"I will always love you and only you," she cooed as his life left him. She leaned over and kissed him on the lips.

Martha's parents truly loved Gertrude. Martha's mother insisted that Gertrude was John's wife and that Gertrude should live with them as part of the family. Gertrude had no other family. Martha comforted Gertrude and helped her get back on her feet. Gertrude did not have to work around the house, but she did insist on helping with the household duties. It was the love she had for Martha's parents that got her through the most difficult part of her life. Gertrude was so grateful. Five years later, Gertrude assisted the doctor in the delivery of a beautiful baby girl named Martha. Joy was back in Gertrude's life again. Joy and despair could not co-exist within her, she'd often think to herself. Gertrude helped raise Martha as if she were her own child. Gertrude was so grateful to Martha's parents. She would tell all that would listen how wonderful Martha's family was. Gertrude loved to socialize with the neighbors. When Martha's parents died, Gertrude had comforted Martha and helped her through this difficult time. Gertrude loved Martha more than she could express and was so proud that Martha was so resilient. Gertrude could see the very best part of herself in Martha.

Gertrude and Martha lived together in the modest mansion once owned by Martha's parents. Gertrude was so happy for Martha.

"Gertrude!" Martha called.

Gertrude's face began to warm, and a small wrinkle of a smile formed on her lips. She had been lost in her own memories.

"Yes, Martha," said Gertrude.

"Are you okay?" asked Martha.

"I'm sorry dear. My mind wanders off occasionally. I'm so happy for you. This Alexander sounds like a real gentleman. I already like him. Now tell me more," said Gertrude. She was distracted, but still heard most of what Martha had said.

"Oh, he is a gentleman. I'm sure that you've seen him. He is the manager of the bank."

"I do believe that I have seen him at the bank. Let's chat some more at the dinner table. The food is getting cold," said Gertrude.

Gertrude, now a woman in her mid-forties looked over at Martha.

"I love you. I'm sure that your mother is happy for you too," said Gertrude.

5

Alexander arrived promptly at 11:00 AM with a beautiful black carriage drawn by four majestic horses. Martha was sitting alone on the porch.

"I've been waiting for ten minutes now!" she said with a smirk on her face.

"Where is your sister?" he said. He expected them both to be on the porch waiting for him. Now he would have to wait, he thought. He always preferred to arrive promptly at his engagements, because arriving early would mean that he would just have to wait.

"My sister? I don't have a sister!" her face shrunk as her eyes narrowed until she remembered. "Oh, yes, you mean my Aunt Gertrude. She's like a sister to me."

Just then, Gertrude – a tall, thin, lanky woman, came out onto the porch. "I do a pretty good job of taking care of myself! I just don't like waiting on the porch for someone that is bound to be late. I'm Gertrude, you are Alexander, now let's go!"

Alexander escorted Martha and Gertrude to the carriage. Alexander could tell that he was going to like Gertrude. He liked her direct, no-nonsense nature. The carriage was clean and comfortable. Martha and Gertrude seated themselves in the seat closest to the front of the cabin. As Alexander entered the carriage, Martha pointed to the seat directly across from her. He hesitated for an instant after looking over at Gertrude and sat on the empty bench. He signaled the driver to go.

The trip to the park was only thirty minutes. Nevertheless, it seemed quite a long time for both Alexander and Martha. Gertrude, on the other hand, was talking non-stop. All Alexander and Martha could do was to exchange shy glances at each other. Both were a bit nervous.

Even so, he noticed how beautiful that Martha was. She exuded confidence, independence and yet an air of loving tenderness. He knew the moment that she directed him to his seat that she was the one, the only one for him.

During the trip Gertrude rambled on from topic to topic, Martha would glance over at Alexander and find him deep in thought or contemplation. She began to see that she actually did recognize him. He was the man that she'd always dreamed of. He seemed confident, independent and genuinely caring.

The carriage pulled up to the city park. Alexander was first to exit. In the most courteous fashion, Alexander held out his hand for Gertrude. She took his hand as she stepped down from the carriage. Next, with the grace of a beautiful swan Martha exited. She didn't wait for Alexander to assist her. He quickly reached for her hand as she was stepping down from the coach. All three of them walked towards the picnic area, Gertrude on one arm and Martha on the other. The picnic was just a few short steps from the bank. The picnic was in full swing when they arrived. There were plenty of friendly people, a band was playing, and there was lots of food.

"I'll see you two love-birds later," said Gertrude, as she made her way to the other side of the park happily talking to every single person that she encountered.

"Well it's just the two of us now," he said with an air of dignity.

"Don't be so sure. Gertrude will keep an eye on us, just to make sure that we don't leave her behind," Martha chuckled.

"I like her. She sure can talk quite a bit. Does she always have something to say?"

"She's usually not talking much when she's chewing or sleeping. She has manners," said Martha chuckling. "She's a wonderful person, though. I am so thankful that she is in my life. She has helped me through some difficult times."

She glanced away as she remembered the pain she felt from losing her parents. She brushed the tinge of the pain away and thought instead of the beautiful day. The smile returned to her face as she continued.

"I love talking with her, even though she's doing most of the talking."

"Are you hungry?" he said with the charm of a young schoolboy.

"Sure!"

They ate and talked all afternoon. They had many things in common. They both loved to sing when no one else was around. They both enjoyed picnics and exploring the countryside, and had a passion for finances.

"Martha, I need to tell you something. I hope that you don't think I'm crazy, but before I ever met you, before you ever started at the bank, I dreamt about you. I know this sounds crazy, and I can't explain it," Alexander said with a somber look on his face.

"It does sound crazy. I felt that I knew you too on the first day that I met you. I couldn't explain that either," Martha admitted.

Just then, Gertrude came running up.

"Let's go. I have to get the chickens in before sunset, or else those dang foxes will get them. The carriage is ready and waiting," said Gertrude.

They strolled over to the waiting carriage. Gertrude practically jumped into the carriage before Alexander had a chance to assist her. She sat in the middle of the rear bench. Martha waited at the carriage entrance, extended her right hand and Alexander graciously obliged. She seated herself in the center of the seat closest to the driver (opposite Gertrude). Alexander entered the coach. Both women sat in the middle of their respective bench seats. If he were to seat himself next to Gertrude, would he be disrespectful of Martha? Did Martha want him to sit with her? Did Gertrude, acting as a chaperone prefer that he not sit with Martha? Before he could choose, both women laughed, and Martha moved over for Alexander. Gertrude was already talking about all the foods that she ate and the latest gossip around town. Neither Martha nor Alexander was able to get a single word into the conversation. As Gertrude went on about the apple pie, Alexander reached to take Martha's hand. For an instant, Martha withdrew her hand, looked over at him and then reached for his hand. It was at that moment that Martha knew that her life was going to change in a way that she hadn't planned. She was both elated and disappointed all at once. What about college, she thought. She loved cultivating her garden of plans for the future. She would carefully nurture them, rearrange them and adjust them until they were just right. Now her garden of dreams was about to change. Just then, as if Gertrude had read Martha's mind, Gertrude said, "Child, only the Lord knows what the future holds. Have faith!"

6

Alexander, Martha, and Gertrude continued to picnic with each other every Saturday over the next few months. Only once did rain threaten to cancel the outing. However, on that day the rain was short-lived and failed to derail the picnic.

Each outing always began with a carriage ride to call on Martha. Of course, Gertrude would accompany Martha to all of the picnics. It was not proper for a woman to be alone with a man without an escort especially one with a budding romance as this. After arriving at the picnic area, Gertrude would wander off and talk with just about anyone that would listen to her. She was never far, and would unexpectedly return for a piece of fruit and then chat with Martha about how good the food tasted. After a few minutes, Gertrude would wander off once again and continue to forage for willing subjects to listen to her latest stories. After a couple of hours of beautiful weather, food, and company – both Martha and Alexander would prepare for the trip home. Gertrude would dominate all of the conversations on the way home. Even so, they all would be laughing and enjoying each other's company. The ride home was never a boring one. Gertrude saw to that. She was a natural at recounting the intricate details of every person that she knew. People always felt comfortable in confiding their deepest secrets to Gertrude. Considered a wise woman among her friends, Gertrude's advice was highly regarded. She would sometimes share some of her observations about the other picnic patrons, but she would never divulge anything that might harm anyone. She truly cared about people.

On one of the outings, Alexander seemed pre-occupied. Gertrude was talking non-stop to Martha. Alexander noticed that Martha was just nodding her head as Gertrude jumped from subject to subject. Alexander tried to interrupt a couple of times, but Gertrude would not yield. Alexander, in a most unceremonious manner, cleared his throat. It was evident to Gertrude that Alexander had something on his mind.

"What's the matter with you, Alexander? If you've got something to say, just spit it out," she said.

Alexander really did enjoy Gertrude's company most of the time, but today he really wanted to spend time alone with Martha. He looked over to Gertrude and said, "Oh isn't that Mrs. Jenkins over there. Didn't you want to talk to her about her chickens?"

Gertrude glared at Alexander while smiling.

"If you want to be alone with your lovebird, why don't you just say so?" she said as she winked at Martha and wandered off to catch Mrs. Jenkins. She didn't wander too far, though.

Alexander turned his attention back to Martha.

Martha's eyes followed Gertrude for a few seconds and turned slowly to Alexander

"Gertrude is quite well aware of your intentions," she said.

"Yes, I know. Martha, I wanted to speak with you about something that is very important," he said with determination in his voice.

"Is something wrong?" she said as her voice cracked. "I thought that everything was going well. What could possibly be wrong on such a beautiful day as this?"

"Of course nothing is wrong. Please come here and sit down for a moment," Alexander said.

"Alexander, now you are scaring me," she said. She walked over to the wooden bench and sat.

He sat next to her and reached for her hand. He was silent for a few seconds as he gazed into her large, beautiful eyes.

"Will you marry me?" he asked.

Martha jumped to her feet. In an instant, those four words hit her straight across the face. What about college? What about all of her plans? What about her future? All of those questions came rushing into her mind. She slowly started to sit down again as she realized that she had fallen in love with this man. She wasn't expecting it. It just happened, she thought with amazement. She turned and faced him The words that Gertrude had said to her on their first picnic outing came to her, "Only the Lord knows what the future holds. Have faith." Martha looked into Alexander's deep brown, tearful eyes and for the first time saw how vulnerable he was. He really does love me, and I love him, she thought.

"Yes," she said with an air of dignity and confidence. "Yes! Yes! Yes!"

She fell into his arms, and they both hugged each other ever so tightly. They didn't notice Gertrude walking towards them with an enormous grin on her face. Gertrude kept uncharacteristically quiet as she stopped just a few feet from them.

Gertrude cleared her throat loudly.

Martha looked up at Gertrude.

"Gertrude. You'll never believe what just happened," Martha said as she waved her hands as if conducting an orchestra.

"What's that?" said Gertrude in a calm, reassuring voice. "Alexander asked me to marry him," said Martha as she wiped away the tears from her cheeks.

"And what was your answer?" Gertrude asked.

"Of course I said yes!" Martha said laughing through her tears of joy.

Just then, a huge clap of thunder rolled through the heavens.

"Even the heavens applaud your decision," Gertrude laughed.

All three of them laughed.

"We must leave now," Alexander said, still laughing. "It's half past three. The rain may start soon."

Alexander escorted the women back to the coach. This time,

without a word, Gertrude extended her arm to Alexander before entering the coach. Alexander gladly obliged. Gertrude sat down in the middle of the backbench. Martha entered next and sat on one end of the front bench. Alexander sat next to Martha. She reached for his hand, and they held hands silently all the way home.

Gertrude had a beautiful smile on her face as she quietly contemplated the bliss that this wonderful young couple had found. She silently planned the upcoming wedding. She already had it all arranged in her mind; she'd dreamed about Martha's wedding for years. She helped raise Martha so of course, she'd help Martha with the wedding. Gertrude knew that Martha would welcome her help.

7

Martha and Alexander had a simple church wedding with only a handful of guests. Gertrude had wanted to have the wedding in Martha's home just as Martha's own parents had some years before. However, Martha and Alexander wanted to be married in the beautiful church that was not far from their favorite park. It was Alexander's idea. He felt that they needed to be married in the church to have a blessed union.

Martha was happy that four of her close friends were there. She'd known them since she was a little girl. All of them still lived in the same neighborhood that she did. Her closest friend was the bridesmaid. She lived in the house next to Martha's home. Alexander's aunt, Gertrude, several of Alexander's friends, the owner of the bank, the other bank manager, several wealthy bank patrons (including Charles and Victoria Adams), and the family doctor attended.

Alexander and the minister were already waiting at the front of the church. Alexander was a little nervous. He was thrilled and excited that he was about to marry the love of his life. He was tapping his foot steadily as he waited for Martha to come up the aisle. This was one quirk of his that he'd never overcome - nervous anticipation. He stopped tapping his foot when he caught a glimpse of Martha's dress through the doorway at the back of the church. Unbridled happiness replaced his impatience.

Martha was waiting at the back of the church with Gertrude. Martha was wearing a beautiful billowy white wedding dress. It was the dress that her mother had used on her wedding day. Gertrude had stitched some beautiful flowers onto the wedding dress and had added even more fullness to the dress than originally was there. It was beautiful. Martha was holding a full bouquet of flowers that Gertrude had picked herself from the garden. Gertrude had braided Martha's long dark hair and pinned it atop her head. She had wispy ringlets of hair softly caressing her temples and the front of her ears. On top of her beautiful head, she wore a simple bonnet. She exuded elegance with an air of nobility and the softness of femininity.

As she stood there in the back of the church, Martha was not as nervous as she'd thought that she would be on her wedding day. She was so thankful that Gertrude had taken care of all of the wedding details for her. The one detail that did bother her was that her father was not there to "give her away" at the marriage ceremony. She'd been crying earlier that morning about it. She told Gertrude that she still missed her parents very much and walking down the aisle without her father would be difficult.

"Martha, there will be no tears of sorrow today, only tears of joy. Your parents are here with you, and I'm sure that your father would want me to walk you down the aisle," Gertrude had said.

Martha looked down at her bouquet and then over to Gertrude.

"I'm ready, Gertrude," said Martha.

Gertrude motioned to the minister that Martha was ready. Gertrude took Martha's hand. They walked up the aisle to an expectant Alexander.

Alexander looked at his beautiful bride as she approached. Then in what seemed an instant later, they were both walking out of the church as husband and wife. He would later recount the details at the picnic:

> "I was standing there looking at Martha. She was beautiful.
> As she walked up, I took her hand. We both faced the
> minister. He asked me if I loved Martha, and if I would
> take care of her and of course, I said that I would. Then he

asked Martha if she loved me if she promised to take care of me. She said she would. Then it was finished. I kissed Martha and then everyone clapped. It was wonderful, but it was so quick. Next, we strolled over to a waiting carriage and here we are."

Martha would later recount the details to Gertrude:

"It was wonderful. I was so happy that you were walking with me down the aisle. I looked over at Alexander. He seemed to be calm and serene. He reminded me of an expectant schoolboy who was obediently awaiting his prize. He was so handsome. I looked over to all of our friends. They looked like a sea of happy faces. I was grateful that they had come. I thought that we would never reach the front of the church. Time seemed to stand still for me. As I approached the steps, Alexander extended his hand to me. It was romantic. I walked over and stood right next to him. The minister asked us if we were ready and we both answered yes together. The minister started with a short prayer. I'm embarrassed to say that I don't even remember what he was saying. I was looking over to Alexander when the minister had cleared his throat. He'd asked me if I'd promise to take Alexander as my husband, care for him and love him with all of my heart. Of course, I said yes. It was wonderful. The minister finally announced us as husband and wife to everyone. Alexander reached over and kissed me. As he kissed me, it seemed like he and I were all alone, far away from everyone. The minister cleared his throat. I was embarrassed. Then, we both looked at our friends, and they were all clapping. Gertrude, it was just wonderful."

Gertrude arranged a very large party afterward in the large clearing behind their house. She'd thought about setting up the party inside of the barn, but quickly changed her mind when she walked in. "Oh, my goodness; too smelly!" Gertrude said with a grin.

She'd managed to borrow enough tables, chairs, and other items from the church for all of the guests. She'd promised the church that everything would be returned in time for the upcoming church social. She enlisted some boys from the neighborhood to help with the setup. Gertrude had meticulously overseen the preparations and setup of the festive event. The eating area was next to the house. There was an area for the band and a nice large area for the guests to dance. On the porch, nearest to the kitchen was the area that would hold all of the food. Gertrude had enlisted a few of her friends to help with the cooking.

Everything was ready when the guests began to arrive. There were over one-hundred-fifty guests. Most of them were Alexander's friends and acquaintances. Most of them were wealthy bank customers. Martha had her four close friends there, one of whom was the bridesmaid. The rest of the guests were Gertrude's friends. Many of them were people that she talked to every single day. In no time, all of the guests had already arrived and were waiting for the happy couple.

When Alexander and Martha arrived, everyone cheered and clapped for the happy couple. The guests were quick to walk over to the couple and personally congratulate them. After fifteen minutes of this, Alexander noticed that Martha seemed to be getting a little overwhelmed with so many well-wishers excitedly talking to her all at once. She loved the attention and the beautiful words from them, but she hadn't eaten all day, and her excitement had kept her wide awake the night before. Alexander raised his right arm in the air to get everyone's attention. Within seconds, the sea of guests went quiet. He was a little surprised that even the band had stopped playing. He laughed and yelled, "Thank you, everyone. Let's eat!"

After just a few more well-wishers had waved their congratulations to Alexander and Martha, the guests made their way to the tables. Within minutes, Gertrude and her friends had served everyone generous portions of the tasty feast. There was chicken, vegetables, bread and much more. Gertrude looked across at the guests.

"This is absolutely delicious," one guest said.

"This is marvelous," said another.

So many guests uttered complements. Gertrude was pleased that everything had gone so well. Gertrude looked over towards the happy couple and saw Alexander escorting Martha to the clearing near the band. The band had just started a lovely song that was Martha's favorite. Gertrude smiled softly as she saw Martha and Alexander dancing.

Alexander was looking adoringly at his wife as they danced.

"Martha, I love you," he said.

"I love you too!" Martha smiled.

Alexander had known that it would work out this way. After all, he had dreamt about meeting and later marrying Martha. He never questioned it. He was just happy that fate was on his side.

8

The happy couple decided to move into Martha's house. Alexander insisted that Gertrude lives with them. He knew that Martha loved Gertrude very much, and he couldn't imagine his and Martha's life without Gertrude. Their new home was much larger than Alexander's home.

"There's enough room for ten children if we wanted," he had told Martha.

The next few months were blissful for them. Alexander continued to work at the bank. Martha had planned to keep working there also, but soon she realized that other duties would need her time and attention. She was expecting her first child. Though it happened quicker than they had expected, both Martha and Alexander were jubilant about this. She left her job at the bank. Her desire to go to college to complete her education was waning. It was 1841, and it was rare these days anyway for a woman to go to college, much less obtain diploma credentials, she thought to herself. Perhaps she was rationalizing why she had let go of her dreams. The joy of bringing a new life into this world felt so gratifying to her. She let her new dreams that were full of so much hope replace her old ones. The new life of hers was rich beyond her wildest expectations. She felt fulfilled as a person. For the first time in her life, she felt powerfully in control of her destiny.

Martha was so excited about being a mother. Alexander would often find Martha singing early in the morning as she went about preparing for her beautiful new child. Her life was wonderful with a lovely husband and soon a beautiful child.

Martha and Gertrude would talk for hours as they prepared the baby's room and gathered the items Martha would need for the baby. When Martha's time came, Gertrude assisted the doctor to deliver a beautiful baby boy, Alex. Although, Gertrude would insist that the doctor helped her.

"He's beautiful," Martha said to Gertrude.

Gertrude brought the newborn to Martha's extended arms.

"Look at his eyes, Alexander. They're barely open. They are beautiful," said Martha.

"He's handsome," said Alexander with a smile.

"He sure is," said Gertrude.

Alexander and Martha were so happy with their new son.

The doctor who was attending Martha when Alex was born was concerned about Martha. He saw that Martha's body had suffered lots of trauma. He knew that Martha had fainted at least twice. She revived sufficiently to complete the birthing process, but the doctor was worried. He'd thought that Martha had died when she passed out the first time. The doctor told Alexander that Martha would not survive if she were to have another child. He told them that this birth had weakened her constitution.

"Ridiculous! Martha is a strong woman," he had told the doctor.

When Alexander later told Martha, she too was bewildered. She said that it was true that she had felt a little tired after birthing their child, but she felt just fine. Surely, the doctor was wrong, they both decided.

After a few days, Martha was up on her feet and back to her usual routine. She excitedly cared for her new baby boy. She loved him, pampered him and adored him. Alexander thought it fitting to name him, Alexander Charles, even though they would call him Little Alex, or just plain Alex. Alexander chose the name Charles for his son's middle name because it was the name of Martha's father. Martha often talked about how her son would grow up to be a banker or an accountant. She knew for sure that he would be great and so did Alexander. They were both very proud of Alex. Alex was a predictable loving baby. He always woke up promptly at dawn's first light. It was almost as if he couldn't wait to get the day started. Of course, for the first several months of his life, he'd wake up and wail to get his mother's attention. Eventually, he would sleep through the night.

During the day, he would nap off and on, but once he turned one, he had the energy to spare. He quickly mastered the art of walking. He exploited this newfound gift by traveling the far reaches of his room and then far beyond the walls of his bedroom. He was not satisfied sitting quietly in his room. His sole mission, he thought was to explore this new frontier known as home.

Alexander was so proud of his son's independence, but Martha was worried that Alex might wander into trouble. Alex had found himself confronted with the perils that plagued their home. Like the time that Alex had seen his mother place a plate of cookies on the table. It did not occur to him to ask for one. He set about on a mission to get a cookie. He made his way to the chair next to the table. He walked most of the way there and crawled the rest. Even though walking would get him to his destination faster, he found crawling to be safer. He stood up next to the chair and leaned over the edge of the seat. It was pressing uncomfortably on his rib cage. He pushed up on the seat of the chair and used his legs to get the rest of his little body firmly planted on the seat. He rested for a minute and then stood up, wobbly at first. He peered over the tabletop and eyed the plate of cookies. He reached over and picked up a cookie - then another and another. He'd already eaten two and decided to head back to his toys. With a cookie in his hand, he made several unsuccessful attempts to climb down from the chair. He whimpered. Just then, his father walked in and saw Alex face down on the chair seat with his little legs dangling over the side. His feet were just inches from the floor.

"Alex, my little cowboy, what are you doing?" Alexander said rather amused with his son. He walked over to him, scooped him up and saw what remained of a broken cookie in his hands and sugar on his face.

Martha ran in, "Oh my goodness!" she saw the cookie dish, the crumbs smeared all over Alex's face, and her son safely in the arms of her husband. She began to laugh.

"My little cowboy, indeed!" Martha said as she hugged them both.

At two years old, he was inquisitive, a phenomenal problem solver and very determined when he was pursuing his goals. As Alex got older, he was extremely curious, always wanting to know why and how things worked.

There was a very special relationship between Alexander and his son Alex. Alex would always wait anxiously by the door for his father to come home. Sometimes he would cry incessantly for his father. When Alexander would walk in the door, he would scoop up his son in his arms. Then he would ask Alex about his adventures that he and his mother had experienced that day. Alex would spare no detail and tell his father all about the wonders of the day.

9

Both Martha and Alexander were avid book readers. They spent time reading almost every day. One day, Alexander brought home a book titled "A Journey to California Guide Book." It was a fast read for Alexander. Each page sparked his imagination with a world of possibilities. He could barely contain his excitement as he read each page. It talked about exploring new territories in the vast unknown of the West. He told his colleagues at work and many of the bank customers about the book. A few days later, he talked with his wife.

"Martha, I would really like for you to read this book. I am sure that you will enjoy it. It is a book about traveling out west."

He knew that she loved traveling.

She put a bookmark in the book that she was reading and put it down. It was about the adventures of Daniel Boone. Only a few more pages and she would have finished it. Now she would have to find another time where she could sit down and read the conclusion of this exciting adventure story.

She smiled politely, still wondering what Daniel Boone was about to do in the last few pages of her book.

She looked at the book that Alexander had in his hand. Martha really enjoyed it when Alexander would latch onto a new adventure. She found his enthusiasm exhilarating and enjoyed living vicariously through his hopes and dreams. However, she did have hopes and dreams of her own. She would continually cultivate and nurture them. She knew that eventually, they would come to fruition into her life in wonderful and creative ways. She wanted him to realize his hopes and dreams, too.

"It's barely more than a pamphlet. Is this what you've been consumed with these last few days?"

Martha was not very supportive, he thought. Now he wasn't quite sure why he had wanted her to read it. Perhaps it was more of a fantasy than an exciting opportunity for him and his family.

"How can you trust such a poor excuse for a book?" Martha said a little cynically.

"Martha, it's a guidebook. There are so many articles in the newspaper, books and yes, pamphlets about those many people who have made the trek out west. We live in exciting times to have a chance to be part of this glorious expansion."

She had not expected Alexander to respond so defensively. She looked over at him and reached out for the book.

"Dear, I'm sorry I didn't realize that this was so important to you. Let me see that," she said.

She began to skim through the book, slowly at first and then turning pages faster and faster as she read on. She sat up as her eyes widened with excitement and then she paused. She looked up at Alexander. He was looking intently at her.

"We have a small child. Will he be safe? For that matter, will we all be safe?" she asked.

"Martha, Alex will be safe as we all will. So many people have made this trek. Several families whose husbands work at the bank have the means to make this journey and really want to. This book says that this is not a journey of endurance, but of excitement, exploration, and liberation," said Alexander.

Martha looked up and realized that Alexander had already made up his mind. She knew that it was common for husbands to make choices for the family without regards to the wishes of the wife. However, she knew that Alexander was different. She knew that if she were to tell him that she would not go, then he would let go of this dream.

"Liberation! Now that might make this worthwhile," she said.

She often talked to Alexander about how stifling it was to be a woman in these modern times of 1843, especially in the city run by men. She was quite adventuresome herself. She feared nothing. She did not like women treated in such a dismissive way.

"Martha, we have the ways and the means to make this trek safely and comfortably. There are neighbors, friends, and loyal bank patrons with whom we could make this trek. All who have traveled to the West agree that it is prudent to go as a group of friends and family, and to outfit each family with sufficient provisions including food, medicine, tools, and spares."

Alexander and Martha would discuss this often over the next few weeks. Each grew to love the idea of leaving the oppression of the big city. They both enjoyed the creature comforts that a big city afforded, but the hustle and bustle of the big city made them ache for the feel of their rural roots. Each of them had grown up in the times where life was a little bit slower. That was when people took their time to enjoy each other's company. Nowadays, everyone was concerned about money and property.

One night after supper, Alex looked up at his father and exclaimed, "Want California!"

"Son, what did you say?" Martha looked over at Alexander and then to their son. Alexander was a two-year-old with an excellent vocabulary.

"Want California!" he yelled and then laughed. He was looking squarely at Martha.

"Well then, we are going to California," Martha said smiling at her son. Then she looked over to Gertrude who had always refused to discuss the subject with Alexander and Martha. Gertrude was a free spirit and believed that it would be best to let things play out "as they should" she would always say. Gertrude was happy wherever she was.

"Gertrude, would you care to join us on our trek to California?" Martha asked.

"I wouldn't miss it for the world," Gertrude replied.

One month into the preparations for the continental trek, Martha found herself again with child. At first, she kept this to herself. Gertrude was the first to notice the change in Martha.

Martha was sitting in the garden where she went to contemplate life's sometimes difficult choices that she occasionally encountered. Gertrude was in the kitchen putting the breakfast dishes away. She wiped her hands on her apron, took a deep breath, and walked casually into the garden.

"It's a beautiful day, Martha," said Gertrude.

"Yes, it is. I love the feeling of the sun on my face. And the cool breeze reminds me how sweet life truly is," said Martha.

Gertrude looked just beyond Martha's shoulder and saw Alex playing with some small wooden toys. He was absorbed in his playing. She could see that he wasn't paying attention to her or to Martha. She walked over and sat next to Martha. Gertrude kept an eye on Alex, lest he hears something that he shouldn't.

"When are you going to tell Alexander?" asked Gertrude.

Martha looked over at Gertrude, "Tell him what?"

Martha was so enjoying the euphoria of the beautiful day in the company of her beautiful child.

Gertrude moved her gaze from Martha's eyes to Martha's right hand that was softly resting on her stomach area. Martha's eyes welled up with joy.

"Oh Gertrude, I'm so happy and scared all at the same time," said Martha.

"I'll tell him. He wants to make this trip. We're nearly ready to go. We will be leaving next month. Many women have made this journey while pregnant. You'll be there to help me through this, won't you?"

"Of course you know I will. Why are you scared?" Gertrude asked.

"We will be away from the city, away from the doctors and away from the safety that it affords," Martha said intently.

"Perhaps you should discuss this with-" Gertrude stopped midsentence. Gertrude saw Alexander walking towards them with a bouquet of flowers in his hand. He stopped next to Martha.

"What!" Alexander exclaimed, dropping the flowers.

Both Martha and Gertrude were startled.

"Alexander, how long have you been there?" she said as she looked down at the flowers lying at his feet.

"Long enough," he said. "Why would you not tell me this amazing news?"

"Alexander, we cannot postpone this trip. Many people are depending on us. Besides, we are almost ready to go. Your beautiful child will arrive after we are living in our new home in California," said Martha.

Alexander knew that it was prudent to listen to his wife. She was always right when it came to practical common sense. Her common sense was one of the many qualities that he loved about her. He paused for a moment.

"I'm jubilant, my darling, and I'm thrilled to once again be a father. I love you," he leaned over and kissed her on her right cheek. He looked across at Gertrude, who was grinning from ear to ear. He knew that Gertrude would help Martha through any rough spots. He bent over and picked up the flowers and carefully brushed off the dirt that marred their brilliance. He handed the beautiful bundle of color and sweet aroma to her.

"I love you dear. I will place an advertisement in the paper to have a doctor accompany us. Perhaps our doctor and his family might be interested in coming with us," he said.

A lone tear rolled down her delicate face and stopped as a warm smile illuminated her face. "I'm so happy," was all that Martha could say.

The family doctor and his family did indeed accompany them on their trip. The doctor insisted that each family outfit their supplies with quinine, opium, whiskey, citric acid, and an assortment of tonics. He knew that there were reports of cholera, dysentery, scurvy, snakebites, and a host of other health concerns with the travelers. Martha herself had done a considerable amount of research about the provisions that should accompany each of the wagons. The food provisions included flour, bacon, dried meats, dried fruits, and dried vegetables. Gertrude insisted that they bring her favorites also: wild plum and crabapple preserves. Alexander wanted to bring his and Martha's extensive book collection, but space was limited. Most of the books had come from the library of Martha's father. Those books were her connection to her beloved father. She loved those books. They each chose a small collection of their favorite books to bring.

A month later, on April 1, 1843, they were on the trail headed west with thirty-one wagons. The trek itself was wondrous. The guidebooks warned about the savages along the way. All of their exchanges with the Indians were friendly. The Indians and the group's families each bartered with treasures and food. Often times the Indians would guide the wagon train through difficult terrains or obscure paths. Martha noticed how beautiful the little Indian children were.

Gertrude insisted that all drink her special lemonade each day. It consisted of citric acid, sugar, a few drops of lemon essence and water.

"The doctor says that this will keep us healthy," Gertrude assured them.

Alexander enjoyed sitting up front with the reins in his hands. He'd never done anything like that before in his life. Martha enjoyed sitting next to her husband with Alex. She was thrilled. Gertrude preferred to sit inside the wagon next to their provisions as if she were guarding them.

Barely a month into the trek Alexander saw something moving atop a large hill. It was too far hard to see since the sun was shining brightly behind the figure. As the wagon train drew closer, he saw that it was a young boy watching them. He was about to point him out to Martha when the boy suddenly vanished. He'd only looked away for an instant. Perhaps it was his imagination, he thought.

They had been traveling for four months already, and everyone was all right. Then one day, they came across a rather large creek that was barely three feet deep. It looked so calm and serene. It was not far from the river. Perhaps as the water level fell, it had left this beautiful pocket of water. Martha and a few of the women decided to cool off in the water. It was a hot day, and the coolness of the still water was refreshing. Within a day or two, each of the women developed a high fever accompanied by relentless vomiting. One of the women succumbed to the illness. Within a few days, the rest of the women recovered well enough to resume the trip. Martha took a little longer to recover. She regained her strength and went back to sitting with Alexander while he drove.

On the first day that she sat with him, Alexander said, "Martha, why don't you take a nap, you look a little tired."

"I'm fine, Alexander," said Martha.

She would sit for a while and then make her way back to a makeshift bed and rest. Gertrude would make sure that she was comfortable.

Alex loved sitting next to his father. When he got tired he would lay down for a nap and snuggle up with his mother.

The wagon train pulled into San Francisco on October 1, 1843. They all cheered as they drove into a large field that Alexander had purchased. There was already a house and a barn on the large patch of land. Their new neighbors were not too far away.

The home was beautiful, Martha thought. She was overjoyed.

"We made it," Alexander said to Martha.

Martha looked up at Alexander. She began to sob soft tears of joy. Her tears quickly turned into a torrent of intense emotion. "I'm so happy, Alexander," said Martha softly.

Alexander picked up Alex and hugged his wife.

Gertrude was crying tears of joy as she patted Martha's shoulder.

10

Alexander, Martha, Alex, and Gertrude settled very quickly into their new home. The doctor prescribed bed rest for the remainder of Martha's pregnancy. He said that because of her recent illness she would require rest until her baby was born. He told her it would only be one more month, and all would be well.

Something was not quite right with Martha. Martha seemed to be tired more often than was usual for her. She often complained about pains, sleeplessness, and strange hallucinations. Gertrude first noticed that Martha was a bit too warm one day. Gertrude couldn't get Martha to wake up, and Alexander was not at home. Gertrude placed a cool cloth on Martha's forehead and ran as fast as she could to fetch the doctor. The doctor lived with his wife nearby. They both arrived to find Martha sitting in the parlor across from her room, crying.

"I've lost my baby!" Martha said sobbing uncontrollably.

"How is that, Martha? The doctor is here to examine you. Let's go back to bed," said Gertrude in a somber tone. Gertrude was scared for Martha.

"Martha, please let me help you," said the doctor.

"Okay," said Martha still sobbing.

The doctor helped Martha to stand and held her tight as he walked her to her room. When they reached her bedroom, the doctor stopped in shock, almost losing his grip on Martha.

"Oh my Lord," Gertrude gasped.

A large stain of blood covered the sheets of Martha's bed.

The doctor led Martha to a nearby chair.

Gertrude quickly gathered the bed linens and whisked them off to another room. She returned with towels, soap, and water and began to clean. Soon, the bed had new linens, and the room was back in order. Gertrude and the doctor assisted Martha back into her freshened bed. The doctor had completed his examination of his patient when Alexander walked into the room.

"What is going on here?" he demanded.

"Sir, may we speak in the next room?" said the doctor.

Alexander saw Martha lying in the bed.

"Martha, are you okay?" asked Alexander.

Martha looked away from him.

"Sir, I must speak with you in the next room," said the doctor as he walked into the hallway.

Alexander took a deep breath and let it out slowly as he followed the doctor into the hallway. They closed the door behind them.

"I'm afraid I have some bad news for you, Mr. Johnson. Your wife has lost the child. It is highly unlikely that she will be able to bear another without grave risk to her life. She had a very high fever and your housekeeper-"

Alexander's eye widened, his teeth clenched.

"She's not the housekeeper! Just tell me what is wrong?" Alexander yelled in desperation. The doctor had been attending Martha for years and he never bothered to notice that Gertrude was part of the family.

"Well sir, Gertrude was not able to awaken her earlier. Your wife was unconscious for a short while. When I got here, she was awake and feverish. We applied cool cloths to her, and now she appears to be feeling better. This is an indication that her fever is lifting," said the doctor.

"Alexander! Alexander!" Martha was screaming in the next room.

Alexander ran back into the bedroom and saw Alex standing just inside the doorway. He was quietly watching his mother, his eyes wide with confusion. While Gertrude was in the kitchen, Alex had quietly crept into the bedroom. Gertrude arrived a few seconds after Alexander and saw panic in Martha's tearful eyes.

"Don't let him see me like this!" Martha screamed.

Gertrude ushered Alex out of the room. Martha put her head down and stared distantly out the window.

"How cruel, how cruel," Martha cried softly as she closed her eyes.

Martha had always been a strong woman. She prided herself on always being ready for anything that life might throw at her. However, this was more than she could bear. How could her God be so cruel to her, cruel to her child, cruel to her family? Her thoughts began to fade into dreamy imagery as she drifted off to sleep.

"She needs to rest now," said the doctor as he walked with Alexander into the parlor. "She will be okay in the morning."

Alexander cleared his throat.

"Yes, Doctor. Thank you," said Alexander.

"Doctor, Martha has been through so much for this child. She wanted this child more than life itself. Perhaps another child could bring her peace. I love my wife so. I can hardly stand to see her like this."

"I understand, Alexander. She is very lucky to have survived this. I'm sorry that she lost the child, but it would be unsafe for her to have another child," warned the doctor.

"I will stop by tomorrow morning to check in on Martha. Please keep her calm and see that she gets plenty of rest," advised the doctor and then left.

The doctor returned the next day and found Martha to be recovering nicely. He visited her several more times over the next few weeks as she continued to improve.

Soon Martha felt her strength returning. Martha was not one to succumb so quickly to tragedy. However, the horror of losing a child, one that she had suffered so much for, was more than she could bear. This was without a doubt, the most difficult assault on her well-being that she had ever endured.

Her mind raced to find the reason for this horrible tragedy. Had I insisted on staying in New York, would this have happened? Was it my husband's fault? Was that filthy watering hole to blame for my loss? These questions haunted her for months as she mourned her baby's death. She hid her suffering very well. To her husband, her child, and Gertrude she displayed love and affection. That was not hard for her since she truly loved them. This is my way of grieving. This horror will stay with me forever.

11

Two years later Martha was once again with child.

"The doctor was wrong," she told Alexander.

This was entirely unexpected, and Alexander was worried for Martha. He thought that she never really got over losing her baby. The doctor was adamant that it would be dangerous for Martha to bear another child. In spite of his worries, God blessed their family with a baby boy, Marcus. Martha was elated.

Marcus was born on March 13, 1845. He was a healthy vibrant child. Martha was surprised at how easy the birthing was.

"It happened so quickly," she told Gertrude.

After a day or two, Martha called for Alex. Alex, already four years old walked in and saw his mother lying in bed, propped up by pillows. She was holding what looked like a bundle of blankets. Alex's eyes widened as he saw the bundle begin to move in his mother's arms and then a wail louder than anything that he'd ever heard came from the bundle.

"I'm here, my baby. It's alright," Martha said to Marcus.

"Come, Alex, meet your new baby brother," she said with such love and affection.

Alex came over, crawled up on the bed and peered into the bundled blankets. He gazed at the baby for a long time and then asked, "Can we keep him?"

"Yes, of course, we can keep him. Since you are his big brother, it will be your responsibility to look out for him and take good care of him. Your father and I will take care of you and Marcus. We love you both very much," Martha said.

"What's his name again?" Alex said nonchalantly. He was pretending to be calm but could barely contain his excitement. Alex was great at maintaining a calm demeanor most of the time.

"His name is Marcus," Martha said to Alex, half-grinning.

"I like that name. I like that name a lot," Alex said.

Martha loved how Alex took such a warm interest in his brother over the next few years. He rarely wandered far from Marcus. Both Martha and Alexander often smiled with pride for Alex. He would spend hours teaching Marcus about life from a child's point of view. He would teach him how to talk, count, draw, walk, get cookies, and all sorts of things. At three years old, Marcus was walking, running and talking.

"It is such a joy to see them together," she told Alexander as she saw them both playing with little blocks of wood that Alexander had made for them.

"Yes, Alex loves his brother. Marcus loves the attention," Alexander responded.

Martha looked away and glanced out the window as if deep in thought. Alexander could sense that something was on Martha's mind.

"Is everything okay?" he said, not quite sure what to expect.

"Everything is wonderful," she paused for a few seconds, "I am with child," she said as her gaze had moved to the floor.

Alexander's eyes widened as he remembered the ominous warning that her doctor had told them just a few years before. She didn't notice his reaction. The doctor's words had also fluttered through her mind.

She looked up towards Alexander. He embraced her and held her tight.

She was so joyful.

Martha was thrilled about having another baby. She was excited, though she felt a little more tired than usual. She was delighted that her two young boys were so inquisitive about the new baby.

"Soon, you will be joined by a baby sister ... or brother," she told them both.

She had been telling them all about how their family was going to grow and how excited that she was that they were going to be blessed with another beautiful child.

"Mommy, how much longer do we have to wait?" asked Marcus. He was always the impatient one. He never understood that sometimes things take time. He had quite a different personality than Alex. Alex was calm, reassuring, and nearly always levelheaded. Marcus, on the other hand, was much more excitable. He was curious about the world around him, just like Alex. However, Marcus was more emotional and tended to cry when things didn't quite go his way. Alex would observe and note. Marcus would observe and react. What a contrast, she thought.

"I love you two so much. Come here," Martha said as she waved Alex and Marcus over.

They ran over to her giggling and laughing all the way.

"We love you too, Mommy," they both said together.

"Now, Mommy's head hurts a little bit, it is time for you two to get to bed," she said as she forced a little smile. She got up from her bed. She ushered them towards the door to her room. The two boys shared a room together and loved it.

"Is father coming home tomorrow?" asked Alex.

Martha looked away to hide a pang of resentment that crept across her face.

"Yes. Your father will be back tomorrow or the next day. He had to go take care of some bank business," said Martha.

Marcus looked a little confused.

"He went to the place where he works," Alex said. "Remember when we went to the bank with Father. That's where he goes every day."

Marcus missed his father too, but it didn't seem to bother him that his father was gone as much as it bothered Alex.

"Oh yes," he said, not really understanding what it all meant.

"Gertrude!" she called from her doorway. "Would you mind helping the children to bed?"

"We can get to bed ourselves. Can Greta tell us a story? She has the best stories," Alex asked his mother.

"Sure, I'm sure she'd love to tell you a story. I'll be there in a moment to give you a good night kiss," her headache was lifting. She loved her two little boys.

Gertrude walked in and whisked the two boys away.

"Now come on you two. I haven't got all night," she said laughing and giggling with them as they walked down the hallway to the boys' room.

"Thank you so much, Gertrude. I'll be there in a few minutes," she said to Gertrude, who was already halfway to the boy's room.

Gertrude looked back with a beautiful, warm smile.

Martha closed her door and sat down on the chair nearest to her bed. She felt that the day was longer than usual. Her headache was lifting, but she felt exhausted. She'd been pretty sedentary throughout the day and hadn't really exerted herself. The last few months had been difficult for her.

She was dozing off when a small knock was at the door.

"Martha, are you okay?" Gertrude said softly.

"Come in, please," said Martha awakening with a little start.

"The boys are asleep. My stories, or should I say gossip about the happenings around this town always seem to put them to sleep before I have a chance to tell them too much," Gertrude chuckled.

"My baby is due soon," Martha said, "and Alexander is not here. What if..."

"Martha, let's get you to bed. You look exhausted. The doctor said that you should get plenty of rest. You know what he said about exerting yourself," said Gertrude. She noticed that Martha's eyes were dark and drooping. Martha's voice was wispy and drawn out.

Martha stood up and made her way back to bed. Gertrude pulled back the covers and helped Martha in.

"Now Martha, remember to call me if you need something. There's no reason to get out of bed unless you really want to. I'll leave the door a little open so that I can hear you," Gertrude said as she walked out of the room.

"Goodnight, Gertrude. I love you so much," she said as she drifted off to a deep, but not a very sound sleep. She started to dream.

> She was in bed, had just given birth to her child and was holding her little baby. Alexander walked into the room and briskly walked over to Martha. She was happy to see him.
>
> "Look, Alexander, we have a baby girl. Isn't she beautiful?"
>
> Alexander said nothing. He walked over to Martha and snatched the infant child from her arms. She struggled to grab her baby back and screamed, "Alexander! Alexander! Give me back my baby!" screamed Martha as she cried uncontrollably.

"Martha! Martha! Wake up," Gertrude yelled as she tried to wake Martha up.

Martha snapped out of her nightmare and sat up abruptly.

"Where is Alexander? Where did he go?" Martha asked.

"Martha, everything is okay. Alexander will be back soon. Just lay back down and rest," Gertrude said firmly.

The distant look in Martha's eyes started to subside. Martha sobbed for another minute and took a deep breath. She let it out all at once. Gertrude tried to smile, but couldn't.

"I'm sorry Gertrude, I had a terrible dream. It was just dreadful," said Martha as she regained her composure.

The early morning sun had started to softly light the room.

Martha laid back down and winced as her head hit the pillow.

"Gertrude, I think that it's time."

12

"Gertrude, Alexander is going to miss the birth of our baby girl. She's coming," she said as she sobbed between waves of discomfort.

"Oh my dear, calm down. I'll go get the doctor," Gertrude said.

"The baby will be here sooner than the doctor could arrive," Martha said with certainty and determination. "You'll have to help me birth this baby."

"Okay, Martha we can do this," said Gertrude.

"I know. The baby is already coming," said Martha.

In no time, Gertrude had everything ready to go.

Martha gave birth to a beautiful baby girl. She was a remarkable sight for both Martha and Gertrude.

"Now you hold on to your baby while I get you both all cleaned up. She is beautiful beyond words. She looks so much like you," Gertrude said with such joy.

Martha took her baby girl in her arms and said, "She is beautiful."

"Martha, will you be okay by yourself? I have to go get the doctor. I'll be gone for just a few minutes," Gertrude said rather anxiously. Gertrude had promised Alexander that she would get the doctor at the first sign that Martha was about to give birth.

"I'll be fine," Martha said weakly.

The doctor arrived just a short while later and found mother and daughter resting. He examined Martha and the baby briefly.

"Martha you two are doing just fine. Gertrude did an excellent job in delivering your baby," said the doctor.

"Thank you, Doctor," said Martha. She'd expected the doctor to again tell her that it was ill-advised to have another child. He didn't. Martha smiled contentedly.

"I'll stop by tomorrow morning to check up on you. Remember to get plenty of rest," said the doctor as he opened the door to leave.

Gertrude followed the doctor out of the room.

Then Marcus and Alex walked in and ran to Martha's bedside. Martha smiled at them.

"Mommy just gave birth to a beautiful baby girl. Her name is Marissa," Martha said to Alex and Marcus.

"Is she staying?" asked Marcus.

"Of course she is," she said as she remembered when she was introducing Alex to Marcus just a few years before.

Martha loved her two little boys, but she had always felt a yearning for a baby girl. The birth of Marissa left Martha fulfilled beyond her wildest expectations. She was so happy to have her little girl. Marissa had beautiful dark hair. Quite a bit more hair than her two other children had when they were born.

Gertrude walked back into the room.

"Gertrude looked at Marissa. Isn't she just beautiful?" Martha said.

Gertrude was bustling about Martha's room putting freshly cleaned clothes back into Martha's dresser drawers. Gertrude walked over and noticed that Martha looked exhausted. Martha had had a rough night that continued well into the morning with Marissa's birth. Even so, Martha was beaming with joy as she held her daughter close to her heart.

"She is absolutely beautiful. She looks just like you," Gertrude said warmly.

"Martha, why don't I take little Marissa and let you get a little bit of rest. I'd love to hold her for just a little while until she falls asleep," Gertrude said.

"Oh Gertrude, what would I do without you?" Martha whispered.

Even a whisper seemed to require more effort than Martha could muster. Martha was exhausted.

Martha kissed her little baby on the forehead as Marissa let out a cooing, sweet little sound. Gertrude gently picked up little Marissa and brought her close.

"Hello, my little angel. Let's let your mother get a little rest. You are so beautiful," Gertrude said softly with so much love.

Martha watched as Gertrude gently held Marissa in her arms. Martha moved one of the pillows over and laid her head back on the other pillow to get some rest. A sharp pain shot through her midsection. She gasped. She took a deep breath and let it out slowly. The joy of holding her baby close to her heart had a soothing effect on Martha.

Gertrude heard Martha gasp with pain. "Are you alright? Do you want me to get the doctor?"

"I'm fine," she lied. "I just need to get some rest. I'm very tired."

"Martha, the birth of Marissa was very taxing on your body. You lost consciousness while you were giving birth. It had been for just a few seconds," said Gertrude. "It was a frightful scare. I thought…"

"Gertrude, don't worry. I'll be okay. I promise," said Martha.

Gertrude forced a smile.

"All right, Martha. Just call me if you want anything. I'll be over here in the sitting room with Marissa," said Gertrude.

The sitting room was adjacent to Martha and Alexander's bedroom. Even with the French doors closed, Martha could watch her baby from her bed. Alexander used to have a desk there where he would spend late nights working. Alexander moved his desk to one of the other rooms in the house so that the baby could be close to Martha. The sitting room had a small crib, a cabinet for clothes, a small couch, and a comfortable rocking chair.

Gertrude closed the French doors and glanced over at Martha. Martha was looking intently at Gertrude.

"Gertrude, where is Alexander?" Martha said rather forcefully.

Gertrude looked down at Marissa and then back to Martha. "He has not arrived yet. I sent word to the bank that you'd given birth. I'm sure he'll be home soon."

Martha pulled up the covers and closed her eyes.

Gertrude thought for a moment, and a twinge of pain crossed through her thoughts. She could plainly see how difficult this birth had been for Martha. Martha had insisted to her that Alexander seemed to her to be turning the two boys against her. When Gertrude would ask her why she thought this, Martha would dismiss the thought. "Perhaps, it is my imagination," Martha would say.

However, Gertrude knew better. The doctor had told her that pregnancies and childbirth were very taxing to a woman's constitution.

"Some women act irrationally," the doctor had told Gertrude.

Gertrude glanced back at Martha. She seemed to have drifted off to sleep.

"Thank goodness," Gertrude whispered.

She looked at Marissa, safely nestled in her arms. The beautiful bundle of joy had fallen asleep. She quietly made her way to the crib and gently placed Marissa inside. Marissa let out a soft sigh, relaxed her tiny body, and drifted off into a sound sleep. Gertrude pulled the little blankets over Marissa's dainty little body. Gertrude peered lovingly at Marissa for a long while. Martha was right. Marissa is beautiful. Gertrude walked over to the rocking chair and drifted off to sleep.

Marissa was not a baby that cried much. Although, there were times that she would be hungry, and that was really the only way Marissa could get her mother's attention. Even so, Marissa was always smiling, laughing, or giggling most of the time. She was a very happy baby. Martha once told Gertrude that God had sent Marissa to help her get through rough times.

By the time that Marisa had begun to walk, she'd practically run towards her mother. She was a little unsure of herself and thought that if she walked too slowly, she would fall. There was rarely a waking moment that Marissa was not with her mother. Martha loved it, although Gertrude would often intercede. She would tell Marissa, "Your mother must get her rest too, little one."

Marissa was walking and talking way before her two brothers had started. She admired her two older brothers. She'd watch them carefully and often mimic their behavior.

"That's probably why she was such a fast learner. She is a keen observer," Gertrude would say.

Gertrude was right. Little Marissa was always watching, always learning, and always trying something new. She seemed to be fearless. She cared little about how things worked. She was more the type to accept what she learned about how things worked as true and then expected things to just work.

By the age of three, Marissa was dainty, strong willed, and very sensitive. Gertrude once told Martha that Marissa reminded her of a beautiful rose. The rose had delicate petals supported by a sturdy thorny stem that stood in the garden for all to admire. Marissa was very sensitive and could easily sense when things weren't behaving as they should. She expected everything to be predictable and was very uncomfortable if they were not.

Marissa especially loved to be near to her mother. Marissa loved watching her mother and mimicking her mannerisms.

13

Although Martha beamed with happiness when she was attending to Marissa, she felt tired. She wasn't sleeping well. Gertrude reminded her that the birth of Marissa was particularly taxing on her body. Gertrude helped Martha to bed one day.

"You need to rest more. I can take care of the house for you," Gertrude told her.

"I'm just so tired all of the time. I'm exhausted," said Martha.

"I notice that you have been getting a bit short-tempered with Alexander lately," said Gertrude.

"He's never around. And when he comes home, he...," Martha would start and then tell her all about Alexander's shortcomings.

As the days passed, Gertrude noticed that Martha grew more and more irritable.

Soon, Alexander and Martha began engaging in serious disagreements that would often end in severe arguments. To Alexander, it seemed that Martha was getting tired of him. She looked fine to him. He'd asked her why she seemed to be always angry with him. She'd just say that he expected too much from her.

"What do you mean?" he would say to her.

Martha remembered the nightmare she'd had where Alexander took her daughter away from him. She remembered the nightmare clearly. It happened right before Marissa was born. She knew it was just a bad dream, but every time that Alexander came home from work, he'd immediately whisk his little baby girl into his arms. Once, he'd even taken Marissa from Martha's arms so abruptly that Martha felt as if she was experiencing her nightmare again.

She didn't want to tell him about this fear. She imagined that he'd tell her that she was crazy for thinking that he would ever take Marissa away from her. Marissa was her very special baby girl that she'd always dreamed of having. The thought of losing her little girl, even to the man that she loved was more than she could bear. The whole thing didn't make sense to her.

Somedays were better than others for Martha. But on a bad day, she would look accusingly at Alexander and scream, "Get out!"

Then the fight would begin. Alexander was bewildered. After a few minutes, he'd see Martha turn from angry to fearful. He couldn't bear to see the woman that he loved with all of his heart become so distraught. If he stayed, he might tell her something that he'd regret.

"I'll let you get some rest," he'd say to her and then leave. Alexander would go for long walks to cool off after the most severe arguments often taking Alex and Marcus. Little Marissa preferred to stay with her mother. Martha would regain her calm quickly as she doted over her baby girl.

Marcus really enjoyed the walks in the country with his father. Sometimes, Alex would ask his father what he had done to provoke his mother. Alex was always concerned about his mother. It wouldn't take too long, though for Alex to become distracted with the beautiful pond that was full of fish, turtles, frogs, and all kinds of critters. He and Marcus would construct little boats of twigs and leaves, and place them in the pond. Alex's boats would always float. The boats that Marcus made would teeter over on their side and eventually break apart as the fish would come up to investigate the object that was floating on the surface of the water. Alexander loved watching his two boys play near the pond's edge. He noticed that Alex would collect the pieces of twigs and leaves that had dislodged themselves from his little brother's boat to instruct Marcus in the proper ways of shipbuilding.

"Marcus, you need to secure each of the leaves on your boats with twigs so that they are tight against each other. And did you forget to make sure that your boat is not too heavy?" Alex said to Marcus.

"Yes, Alex. I tried!" Marcus retorted. Marcus was discouraged but didn't really care since he didn't have the same interest in boats that his brother did. Marcus enjoyed throwing rocks in the water, mostly at the fish. He never would hit any fish, but it was fun anyways.

Alexander, Alex, and Marcus would stay by the pond for hours talking and playing. It was fun for the two boys. It was peaceful for Alexander. By the time that they got home, Martha would already be in bed. Alex was the first to notice that Martha had begun to withdraw more and more from her family.

Alexander would often be gone for two weeks at a time while he conducted banking business in neighboring towns. He seemed to volunteer often for these types of assignments. Martha knew this, he had told her. He found that his desire to be around Martha was diminishing. Likewise, Martha seemed to be happier when he was gone. Alex would notice how unhappy his mother was and thought that maybe his father was the cause of his mother's unhappiness.

Soon, Martha began to have frequent nightmares. She would wake up crying and drenched in sweat. Since Alexander was gone most of the time, Gertrude would rush into Martha's room to comfort her. Gertrude became alarmed one day when Martha asked her why she'd taken the children to the church picnic without her the previous week.

"Martha, what are you talking about," Gertrude said. "We haven't been to a church picnic in years."

Martha looked confused. Then she covered her mouth and laughed. "Oh Gertrude, I'm sorry. I had an awful dream where you, Alexander, and the children left me here alone. It was a terrible nightmare."

"Well, Martha, you can be sure we'll all be going to a church picnic together when you get better," Gertrude said.

A few days later, Martha heard Gertrude telling Alexander about the episode. Could Gertrude be turning against me? Martha thought.

Gertrude continued to take care of the children and the house. She was cooking all of the family meals and doing most of the chores around the house that Martha used to do. Martha preferred to stay in her bedroom. Alex would insist on bringing meals to his mother in her room. Martha enjoyed her son's company. They would talk for hours. He sat in the chair beside the bed where Martha would be resting. They would talk about many things. Mostly Alex would tell his mother about how he planned to grow up to be a sailor on the open seas. He would tell her all about his ship building exploits. Alex learned long ago, never to discuss his father with his mother, as she would immediately dismiss him.

"I've got a headache! Please excuse me, my dear son," she would say at the mere mention of his father. "I need to get some rest."

Alex once asked his mother why she hated his father so much.

"I don't hate your father. Wherever did you get that idea?" she said. "Now, please let your mother sleep. I'm tired." Martha didn't hate her husband, she thought. She was convinced that he had lost his feeling for her.

"Mother, I love you very much," he said to her, hoping that she would ask him to stay a little longer. She would just close her eyes and say nothing.

Alex would leave the room and look for Marcus. They would play for hours at a time. Alex and Marcus were so different from each other. Marcus was impatient, confident, and very matter-of-fact about everything. Alex, on the other hand, was guarded, quiet, and patient. Both had an aptitude for numbers. The two boys thought that Marissa was much too young to play with. Gertrude would spend most of her time with Marissa. Alex would often say that Marissa was too noisy and that his mother was trying to rest and could not possibly do so with Marissa fussing about.

Martha spent more and more time in bed. She would often send for the doctor. The doctor would prescribe some sort of tonic that was supposed to alleviate her tiredness. It didn't seem to help much.

The doctor had long suspected that Martha was deteriorating because she was wasting away in bed and was at risk of developing pneumonia. The tonics that he'd prescribed to her could help her only if she went for walks. She had never quite recovered from the birth of Marissa. The doctor told her that it was time for Martha to get out of bed and get moving around. Martha ignored the doctor's direction and continued to stay in bed.

Alexander did not take the doctor's direction so lightly. One morning he and Martha argued about it. They had a terrible fight. Both were screaming at each other. Martha was in bed, and Alexander was across the room. Alex was standing near the door. He heard everything. Alexander told Martha that she needed to become part of the family again and that she was very selfish. Martha accused him of caring little for her and spending time with some other woman while he was on bank business. Of course, this was not true, but Martha was not thinking clearly. He left shortly after noon and told her, "When I get back, you'll get out of this bed and assume your role as mother and wife."

After his father had left, Alex went into his mother's room.

"Are you okay?" he asked.

"Yes dear, I'm fine. Please let me get some rest. I'm feeling rather tired."

"Yes mother," he said. He knew that she did not want to talk. He could tell that she was upset. He felt helpless. He wanted to help his mother, but he didn't know how. He went outside and just sat on the swing on the back porch. His world was breaking into many tiny little pieces, and he did not know what he could do to fix it. He felt responsible. A few hours later, Gertrude called, "Dinner is ready, come and get it."

Dinner was unusually quiet with just Marcus, Marissa, Gertrude, and Alex.

As Alex ate, thoughts began to whirl away in his mind. Where is Father? Why was Father fighting with Mother? These were big issues for a young boy to be dealing with.

The next morning, Martha was sleeping longer than usual. Alex tiptoed into the bedroom with a breakfast tray. He called out to his mother as he placed the breakfast tray on the table next to the bed. She did not answer. He looked across at her and noticed that his mother's face looked very pale. He called to her once again. She didn't move. He reached for her hand, and it was icy cold. He remained motionless for a moment until he realized that something was terribly wrong. He called out to her again. She didn't answer. He ran to get Gertrude. Martha was dead.

Alexander was not due back until later that day. He'd told Gertrude that the banking trip was to a nearby town that was about twenty miles away. Gertrude took Alex to the back porch and called to Marcus and Marissa who were playing outside.

"Alex, take care of your brother and sister while I go get the doctor," she said to Alex.

Gertrude made the necessary arrangements and sent word to Alexander to come home. Alexander arrived at his home about an hour later.

Alexander blamed himself. He was distraught and full of guilt. "It's my fault! I told her that she was selfish," he muttered to himself.

Alex was in the doorway listening intently to every word his father spoke. Alex was horrified and speechless. He looked over to his father and then over to his mother's lifeless body and then back to his father.

Could it be true that my father has taken my mother away from me? Alex wondered. He looked over to his father as Alex silently approached the bed. Alexander was so consumed with guilt that he hadn't noticed Alex enter the room and come to stand at the foot of the bed. Alexander was sitting on the side of the bed facing the lifeless body of his lovely wife.

"Father, why did you do this?" said Alex.

"What are you doing in here?" he yelled in a voice that was so full of guilt and anguish. Alex lost his footing and fell back in terror. He saw his father get up and come towards him. Alex jumped to his feet, eyes wide open and ran out the door and flew down the stairs. He lost his footing on the very last step and fell headfirst onto the landing. His head was throbbing with pain. He opened his eyes and saw his father standing over him. Then all went dark for Alex.

Alexander carried Alex over to his bed, "Gertrude!"

Gertrude came running. "What happened?"

Gertrude sat down on the bed next to Alex. She examined his arms, his legs, his neck and finally his head. "He's got a big bump on his head. I'll call the doctor to be sure, but he looks okay. Nothing is broken."

Alex struggled to open his eyes and focused on Gertrude.

"Greta," said Alex.

He'd always called her Greta.

Gertrude remembered that Alex had called her Greta when he was first learning to talk. That was such a long time ago, she thought.

"Yes, Alex. I'm here. How do you feel?" Gertrude said calmly.

"My head hurts a little bit," he said as he started to sit up. He lifted his body with both of his arms and sat up in bed. He turned to look up and saw his father standing behind Gertrude. His eyes widened, his mouth contorted and then he gasped.

"What's the matter, son? Are you okay?" said Alexander.

14

Life continued in the household as the years rolled by. Gertrude cared for the children while Alexander was off on bank business. The children loved Gertrude. She was happy to care for them all. As time moved on, Alex began to withdraw more and more into his studies. He continued to build his boats and imagine that he was on the open seas enjoying the life of a sailor. He had never been on a ship in the ocean before in his life, yet he dreamed for that kind of adventure. He read many adventure books about ships, shipbuilding, and sailing on the open seas. At fourteen, he began to notice the girl who lived down the road from him. He thought that she was pretty, but could never seem to build up the courage to talk to her. She never showed much interest in him, so he never asked her to a picnic.

Alex avoided his father. He would only speak to him when he felt it necessary to do so. Alex would never think of disrespecting his father. However, when Alex thought about the morning that he had found his mother's lifeless body in her bed, it would rekindle his feelings of distrust for his father. He still blamed his father for his mother's death. When Alex thought about these things, he'd turn quiet and distant.

Marcus could usually snap Alex out of his dark mood.

"Alex, what's the matter?" Marcus said with a look of panic on his face.

"Nothing, Marcus. I was just thinking about stuff," said Alex.

"Let's go to the creek and catch us some fish," said Marcus.

"I'm not really feeling up to that right now. Can we do that tomorrow? I've got a lot of chores to do before father gets home."

With that, Marcus would go off in search of Marissa. Marcus was already ten years old, and Marissa was barely seven. "Not much fun with a baby," he'd say to her, but he thought that her company was better than playing alone. Marcus hated to be alone. He was always hanging around someone. He was a boy through and through. He loved to get dirty, climb down the hillside, and sometimes wade in the creek. The creek was barely a few inches deep this time of year. There was not much chance of catching any fish there, except maybe a tadpole or two.

Marissa adored Marcus. She would laugh and play with him all day long sometimes. Anytime that Marissa was with Marcus, it was a certainty that they both would be crawling around in the dirt looking for small unsuspecting bugs. Marcus especially enjoyed sharing his captured bugs with her. She enjoyed the feel of the bugs squirming in her hand. She would pick up a lizard, play with it for a while and then stuff it in her pocket. She had large baggy pockets, and the lizard would easily escape within seconds. One time, Marcus and Marissa were playing in the fields near a tree house that their father had built for Alex several years before. It had a couple of benches and a long table. Marcus and Marissa had been playing there for over an hour. Marcus had fallen asleep on the bench. He woke up soon afterward with all sorts of bugs crawling on his arms, legs and face. They were harmless bugs: pill bugs, beetles, and other small critters. He jumped to his feet and flung his arms about trying to get rid of all of the bugs. Marissa was holding her sides laughing at the spectacle.

"Where did all these bugs come from?" he asked nearly out of breath.

"I've been saving them in my pocket. I thought that these little creatures might like to wake you up," Marissa said.

He laughed and brushed the last of the bugs off his clothes and said,

"Marissa, let's go home. I think it will be supper time soon."

They both climbed down from the tree house and made their way back to the house. Marcus would occasionally find another bug crawling down his back or up his leg and just brush it off. He was not afraid of bugs, but they seemed to be more of a nuisance to him today. Marcus still felt rejected by his brother.

Marcus and Marissa would spend many such afternoons together playing with each other. Alex was already growing up and preferred to spend his time with children closer to his own age.

Over the next few years, Alex continued to grow more distant from the rest of the family. Alexander had noticed that Alex would spend most of his time in the company of his friends. Some of the boys that Alex would hang around were sometimes a little too rowdy. Alexander never talked about his concerns with his son. Alexander was always too busy with bank business. That was what Alex thought about his father.

One night with the full moon shining brightly, the boys stole some bottles of whiskey from the saloon on the other side of town. Alex never had drunk alcohol in his life. Alex and three other boys found an empty barn on a piece of land not far from Alex's home. They all went up in the hayloft and rolled their cigarettes and began to smoke and drink their stolen whiskey. They were having a great time. Not a one of them noticed that an old man had entered the barn holding a lantern and a shotgun.

"Who's up there?" yelled the old man from the entrance to the barn.

At once, the boys went silent. They snuck down the ladder and not so quietly ran out the back. The old man fired his shotgun in the direction of the commotion.

"Get the hell off my property, you dang varmints," screamed the old man.

They were lucky that the buckshot had missed them. The old man went up to the hayloft, discovered a smoldering cigarette and put it out. By then the boys had already disbanded, and each had gone their own way. Alex was on his way home, swaggering all the way. As he approached the front gate to his home, his father confronted him.

"Alex, what are you doing out at this hour?" asked Alexander.

"I was just having some fun with my friends," he slurred back to his father.

"You've been drinking! What is wrong with you? Why have you been drinking?"

"You drink, don't you? Why shouldn't I?" Alex blurted out.

Alexander stood there dumbfounded. He didn't know what to say. His son had never done this sort of thing before.

"I thought that you were better than this. Where have you been?" asked Alexander.

"We were at that old barn up the road," he replied drunkenly. "Some crazy old coot chased us out. He shot at us with his dang shotgun."

"You are lucky to be alive. Why would you do such a thing as this?"

"Since when do you care what happens to me... or to anyone else?" Alex said as he stumbled forward.

"What? What are you talking about?" Alexander was tired from a long day at the bank and was growing impatient. "Get yourself put together and get to bed, son."

"I'm sick of you, FATHER!" Alex yelled in a drunken stupor. "You are a pathetic excuse for a father. I watched you kill my mother and now you stand here and tell me to get myself put together. I hate you! I hate you, you selfish, pompous bastard!"

At that, Alexander raised his arm to strike a blow across his son's face. He couldn't bring himself to hit his son. Instead, he turned around and muttered: "You're just like her, you drunken fool!" Alex clumsily stumbled around. He lost his balance and fell to the ground. In a fit of rage, Alex got up and lunged at his father with all of his might. Alexander fell to the ground. He hit his head on a large rock that nearly knocked him unconscious. Alex began to pummel his father's half-conscious body. Alex was full of all the rage and fury that he had buried since his mother's death. He had concealed his hatred for his father for all these years, but no longer. Alexander managed to get back to his feet for just a moment and fell back down.

"You murdering bastard! You killed my mother!" Alex screamed at his father.

Marcus and Marissa came running out of the house.

"Father, Alex?" Marcus asked.

Marcus was confused. He saw his father lying on the ground bleeding, and Alex was stumbling about screaming: "You killed her!"

Alex looked over to Marcus and then to Marissa and then at his father. Marissa was quietly sobbing. Alex had a moment of clarity about what he had done. He turned around and ran silently down the road. Gertrude was running out of the house as she saw Alex disappear into the night.

"Gertrude, Father is hurt!" said Marissa as she ran to her father. She wiped away the tears from her face.

"Father, are you okay? You're bleeding," said Marissa.

"I'm okay. Marcus, help me get up," said Alexander.

Both Marcus and Gertrude helped Alexander get up. They went inside. Alexander sat in the chair nearest to the fireplace and said, "Marcus, Marissa, please go to bed. Everything will be okay in the morning. Gertrude, will you get me something to clean this mess up?"

Gertrude brought him some water and clean cloths and said, "Alexander, why don't you go get him before he hurts himself?"

"Goodnight, Gertrude! He'll be fine!" Alexander said abruptly.

Gertrude excused herself and made sure that the children were back in bed before going to bed herself.

Alexander sat in the parlor alone staring into the fireplace. He took some deep breaths and then started to cry silently.

"Why?" he asked quietly. He loved his son. Gertrude had told him ever since Martha died that Alex had never grieved his mother's death. Alexander had tried a few times, usually after supper, to talk to Alex about his mother, but Alex would change the subject. He'd say, "It's late, Father. I'm tired. I'd like to go to bed."

Alexander was often away from home for days at a time conducting bank business, so it wasn't very difficult for him to avoid dealing with the issues that were bothering his son. Alexander knew that his son had had a rough time since his mother died. Why had Alex behaved so violently towards him? Was he full of that much rage? Of course, his son was drunk. He knew that Alex had never drunk before. He thought that maybe he and his son could work it all out in the morning. He made his way to the desk in the sitting room and started to look through a stack of letters that Martha had written to him long ago.

"My Dearest Alexander, I love you so much..."

He read letter after letter and then reached over and shut the lamp off. He sat in darkness and for a while gazed out the window until the peacefulness of the night enveloped him.

"Why, my dearest son? Why, my little cowboy?"

15

Alex ran back to the barn where he and his friends had been drinking. He climbed up to the loft and looked around. Though it was a full moon, it was quite dark inside of the barn. He shuffled around the loft until he heard a loud clank of his shoe hitting a bottle. There was still a bit of whiskey left in the bottle. He leaned over to pick it up and then slouched over and fell down. He put his hands over his face and started to cry. A few minutes later, he cleared out a little space on the floor, made himself comfortable on the hay, and fell into a deep sleep.

Alex was dreaming about his mother when he felt something nudging him awake. He could barely open his eyes.

"What are you doing here?" the old man said.

Alex, just laid there not quite knowing where he was. He tried to stand up, but lost his balance and fell back down. He was having trouble focusing. He felt dizzy and disoriented.

"Who are you?" said the man.

"Alex," he whispered, barely able to speak.

Alex looked up and saw the old man pointing a shotgun directly at him.

"I'm sorry sir. I just fell asleep. Where am I?" Alex slurred.

"Get up and get out of here, before I load you up with buckshot, you drunken fool," the old man yelled.

Alex got up and made his way down the ladder. The man continued to yell something at him that he could not quite understand. Alex continued down the road and paused to sit on a rock a while to think about what to do. He thought about going home, but he just knew that his father would not welcome him. He couldn't remember everything that happened, but he knew that he had fought with his father. He knew that it was bad since he had dried blood on his fists and on his clothes. He walked along the road towards his home.

Back at the farm, the farmer went into the barn and took one last look around. He walked outside and closed the barn door.

The light of the moon was so bright, the farmer thought. There were three more hours before sunrise. With all of this commotion, he thought he could go back to sleep at least for a little while before sunrise. He made his way back to the house and went to bed.

Meanwhile, Tom snuck back to the farm to teach the farmer a lesson. Tom had seen Alex leave, and then the farmer walk into the house.

Tom crept out of the barn and snuck to the front porch of the farmer's house. He found the lamp hanging near the front door. The lamp was still warm to the touch. He carefully removed the lamp and ran back to the barn. He opened the door and lit the wick. He threw it into the open barn door and ran in the direction where Alex had gone.

Within minutes, the farmer came running out of his house. The animals were again causing a commotion. He could see the flames coming from the barn through the half-open barn door. He ran to the barn and flung the barn door wide open. In the middle of the barn was his wagon engulfed in flames. He ran in and used all of his might to roll the wagon out towards the courtyard. He pulled and tugged until the wagon began to move. The flames were threatening to spread to the rest of the barn. With only seconds to spare, he expended the last bit of his strength to pull the wagon. The wagon began to move swiftly towards the house. The house was downhill from the barn. He jumped out of the way, as he saw the wagon rolling straight towards the side of his house. The wagon was out of control, and within a few yards of his house, the wagon turned slightly and veered towards the creek. It crashed into the creek with a thunderous clash of wood and metal hitting the fresh water. The water doused the flames instantly. The farmer fell to his knees and thanked God that his house and his barn were safe.

Alex approached his house and found only darkness.

His father had dozed off while sitting at his desk in the sitting room near the front of the house. Alexander woke up when he heard the animals stirring outside. He looked out of the window and saw Alex walking up to the front gate. The full moon illuminated the road outside his home. Alexander thought for a moment and decided that it would be best to leave Alex alone and talk with him in the morning. Alexander made his way to bed and felt relieved that his son had come home.

Tom wanted to make sure that Alex had not seen him toss the lamp into the barn.

Alex was at the front gate of his house when he heard someone calling to him.

"Alex! Alex! What are you doing out here?" said Tom. He was not quite yelling, but calling loud enough to startle Alex.

Alex turned around. He recognized Tom.

"Not much. I don't feel so good," Alex said in a loud whisper.

"Why don't you come over to my house? It's just up the road a bit. I've got something to take care of that," the boy said.

Alex looked towards his house and then back at Tom. "Okay," he said.

They walked down for what seemed to Alex to be an hour or so to a house on a large farm. Alex saw horses, cows, chickens, and a big barn as they approached the house. They snuck in through the back door. They walked into the kitchen. The boy poured something into a small glass. "Here drink this. It'll make you feel better."

Alex reached for the glass and drank it all down all at once. It was hard going down his throat. Within minutes, his head began to settle down. "What was that?"

"Homemade whiskey," Tom said.

"Are you in some sort of trouble?" asked Tom. He had met Alex just a few days before, so he really didn't know much about him.

"No, not really, I just need someplace to go for a while," Alex said. He was making it up as he went along. His head was still hurting, but the shot of whiskey helped to steady him a bit.

"I'm heading to my uncle's house for a little while. He's the sheriff of a town not too far. It's about a day's ride. Why don't you come along?"

Tom thought that it would be better to keep an eye on Alex. In the open country, he could easily dispatch Alex if he'd seen him set fire to that old coot's barn.

"Are you sure that it's okay with your uncle?" asked Alex, not quite knowing what he was doing.

"Sure, I go there all the time," said Tom.

"I don't have any clothes or money," Alex said ashamedly.

"That's okay. You can borrow some of my clothes. We're about the same size. My uncle will treat us real good. Don't worry about it," said Tom.

Alex still could not remember the boy's name. He thought that it might have been something like Tom or Thomas.

"So, what is your uncle's name?" Alex asked.

"He's Sheriff Thomas James Buchanan. I'm named after him," Tom said proudly.

Alex hesitated for a moment and then relaxed. He remembered his name. He thought about what it would be like to travel with Tom to another town for a while. It would be quite an adventure. He figured that he had nowhere else to go. His father would never allow him back home. He wanted to get as far away from his father as he could. Feelings of hatred and rage flooded through him like molten iron as he thought about his father. He really wanted to get away. He wanted to run away. The thoughts of freedom and liberation were exhilarating. He started to feel better. Alex and Tom talked until they heard the rooster announce the beginning of a new day.

"Are you hungry? My mother is out feeding the chickens. She is getting ready to fix some tasty eggs, bacon, and bread."

"Sure thing," Alex said. His appetite was coming back.

Tom's mother walked in.

"Hello, Tom! Who ya got there?" asked Elizabeth.

"This is Alex. He and I are headed to Uncle's place in a little while," said Tom.

"Good to meet you, Alex," she said. "Do you live around here?"

"Yes ma'am," he said.

She had expected him to offer up a little more information. Alex didn't notice Tom glare at his mother. She knew that it would be better for her to stop asking questions. She really didn't care to know where this boy lived. He was probably running from the authorities, she thought.

"Well, you boys better get cleaned up. You stink like you've been carousing with the cows and pigs. I'll get some breakfast for you two. Don't be long," Elizabeth said.

She had long since disapproved of the life that her brother, Thomas, led. He was a sheriff, but she didn't trust him. Growing up he was the meanest and cruelest person that she knew. She and Thomas grew up in this very house. She always resented him for stealing money from their parents and for bullying the kids in the neighborhood.

"He's crooked," she would say to her parents.

"Just have a little patience," her mother would say to her. "He's just trying to find his way."

"But Mother, he's stolen that money you were saving," she would tell her Mother.

Now it was just she and her son that lived there. Her parents had died long ago.

You'd think that a sheriff would have more sense, she thought. At least her brother took good care of her and her son Tom ever since she became a widow some ten years before. Her brother would send more than enough money for them to live on. Perhaps he feels guilty for killing my husband, she thought. Tom seems to admire him quite a bit, she thought. She'd decided that it was better to just shut up about her brother and let things be. She was happy that Tom worked hard on their farm and helped her brother too. She was very proud of her son. Even though he was a bit rowdy at times, he was a hard worker. She put plates of food on the table for Tom and his guest and went to the barn.

It didn't take long for Alex and Tom to get cleaned up. The water was too cold for Alex, but it certainly did help to sober him up. They found plates of food at the kitchen table.

"This is delicious," Alex mumbled around a mouthful of bread and eggs.

They ate until they couldn't eat anymore.

He had food in his stomach, and he had a very attractive offer.

"This will be great! I have wanted to get away from this stinking town for a while now. It would be a great adventure to see what's out there," said Alex.

Tom took Alex to the barn and pointed to one of the horses.

"That horse is for you," said Tom.

"For me?" said Alex not knowing what to say.

"Yes! He's a great horse. You'll love him," said Tom.

They packed the horses and began their journey to a small town that was less than a day's ride away.

It didn't take much to convince Alex to leave. He must really be in some sort of trouble, Tom thought.

16

Alexander woke up with a start. He fought against his aches and pains to get up, his head still sore from hitting the rock. He felt disoriented as he made his way down the hall with a slight stagger. All the bedrooms were empty. The kitchen was empty. He stood near the front door. He didn't notice his daughter in the front room. Marissa was sitting in the chair on the other side of the fireplace.

"Alex!" he yelled.

"He's not here. I can't find him anywhere," said Marissa.

"Of course he's here. He's probably sleeping on the front porch," Alexander told Marissa, confident that he would find Alex there.

"No. Alex is gone," Marissa whispered. She started to cry softly.

It was true. Alex was gone. A feeling of dread enveloped him. Alex was full of so much rage. Why hadn't he mourned his mother's death? He remembered how he'd blamed himself for Martha's death. These thoughts were whirling around Alexander's head. Perhaps he should have spent less time at the bank. Gertrude spent more time with his children than he did, he thought.

Alexander walked up the road and spoke with his neighbors. No one had seen Alex. He went from home to home. He was about to give up. He walked up to a house that was on the far side of the creek. It was a dilapidated un-kept house. He walked towards the front door and heard someone calling from the barn.

"What do you want?" yelled the old man.

"I'm looking for my son," Alexander said.

The old man looked at Alexander suspiciously. He noticed that this man looked very much like the boy that he'd found asleep in his barn the night before. He didn't answer right away.

"My son is about yeah high," he said as he held his arm a little higher than eye level. Alex was nearly as tall as his father was. "He's got lighter color hair, and he's a very good-looking young fellow."

"Sounds like the young man that was sleeping in my barn early this morning. I chased that varmint off my property. He seemed to have a bit more manners than those other mischievous boys that he was with last night. I found whiskey bottles up in the loft. They must have been having a good old time," said the old man.

"He almost burned my barn when he left. I got to it before it got out of control, but not before it destroyed my only wagon," the farmer muttered.

"I'll be glad to provide you with a new one," said Alexander.

"That would be good, sir. The boy did not appear to be the kind of young man to do such a thing, but judging by the kind of company he keeps…"

The farmer's voice trailed off in thought and then continued.

"Two or three other boys had been carousing with him earlier. I chased them all off. A couple of hours later I found your boy here. He said that his name was Alex. That's when I chased him off. I made my way back to my house and was just about to go to sleep when I heard a commotion in the barn. I looked out the window and saw your boy running down the road in that direction," said the farmer as he pointed in the direction of Alexander's home. "He must have doubled back."

The farmer continued, "I started to run after him with my shotgun, and found flames coming from inside the barn. My old wagon was on fire. The flames hadn't spread beyond the wagon, thank goodness. Otherwise, I would have lost my animals. Anyhow, I grabbed the yoke and pulled the wagon with all of my might. It wouldn't budge at first until I noticed that I had put some large stones in front of the wheels.

As soon as I cleared those, it was easy to pull the wagon. The flames were fierce."

"How did the wagon end up in the creek?" asked Alexander. The creek was behind the house.

"I was lucky. Once I got the wagon moving out of the barn, it started barreling towards the house. I tried to reach it from behind, but the flames overwhelmed me. The wagon looked like a huge fireball of burning wood. Just as it reached the path...," the farmer said as he pointed to the path leading to the front door of the house, "...the right front wagon wheel broke and the whole darn thing veered away from the house and crashed into the creek. That creek is so full; it was no time before that dang fire was out."

"I'll help you get that wagon out of the water," Alexander said. He didn't know what else to say. It sounded like the farmer was excited about the whole thing. He didn't seem angry or even upset.

The farmer began to laugh. He'd been speaking non-stop and barely gave Alexander much of a chance to say much.

"Not too much excitement happens here, until last night. I've hated that dang wagon. I spent more time fixing that darn thing than using it. It was taking up space in the barn anyway. And you should have seen me. It was such a thrill!" said the old man.

"But..." Alexander trailed off. He was definitely confused. What in the world was wrong with this farmer, he thought.

"Did he say where he was going?" asked Alexander with both disappointment and a glimmer of hope.

"Nope, I just told him to keep on walking. He didn't look too good," said the old man.

"Which way did he go?" Alexander asked again.

"I just told you. Your boy was running that way," the farmer pointed again in the direction of Alexander's house.

"Thank you for your help," Alexander said.

Alexander turned around and started walking briskly towards his home. He thought that Alex must have decided to go home after the old man ran Alex off his property. He was relieved. He loved his son very much, and he thought that he would talk to his son with understanding. Alex was probably already on the porch swing talking to Gertrude. Alexander often found them together talking on the porch. He sped up his pace, began to forget about the night before, and started to smile. "Yes!" he muttered to himself. "I'll take some time off from the bank and spend some time with my son. Why didn't I think of that before?" he said.

Alexander came around the corner; he could hear Gertrude's loud voice. She was swinging on the porch with someone. Tears welled in his eyes as he began running. The bushes and the tree in the front yard obscured most of the front porch. He had planted those shrubs and trees for the express purpose of providing privacy for when he and his wife were enjoying some private time on the porch swing. Since then, they had become overgrown.

Alexander saw Marcus and Marissa sitting beside Gertrude.

"Where's Alex?" he asked.

A look of sadness crossed Gertrude's face. "He's gone," she said.

"But..." he trailed off into silence.

At that very moment, Alexander's face changed, his body began to slouch. He knew that something must have happened after he'd seen Alex at the front gate. Otherwise, Alex would have been home. His breathing became shallow as he sighed, "Is breakfast ready Gertrude?"

"Yes, it's ready," Gertrude said in a monotone lifeless voice.

Gertrude knew that Alex was gone. She could sense it in her bones. Alex had told her on more than one occasion that he would run away someday. However, she would always convince him to have patience. She would promise him that it would all work out. She would tell him that things happen for a reason, and sometimes life is painful. It would not always be like that. She would tell him that his whole life was just waiting for him. Gertrude hesitated for a moment with that thought and then said a prayer for Alex. He'll be okay, she thought.

17

The sheriff was on the porch as Tom and Alex rode up.

"I was beginning to think that you weren't coming," said the sheriff.

"Hello, Uncle! I brought a friend to stay with us for a while. He's from the city. His name is Alex," Tom said, happy to see his uncle.

The sheriff looked at Alex.

"Welcome, Alex! What brings you to these here parts?" the sheriff asked jovially of Tom's friend.

"I'm just passing through, maybe looking for some work," Alex said, not quite sure of himself.

"Well, you can stay here for a while, that is..." the sheriff hesitated, "...if you take care of the animals, I'm sure we can work out an arrangement," the sheriff said.

"Yes, sir, I'll be glad to do what I can around here," Alex said with more confidence.

The sheriff eyed him and then turned towards Tom.

"Take care of Alex. Put him in the back room. I'll be home later," the sheriff said. "Tom, don't forget about our hotel business."

"I haven't forgotten," said Tom.

Alex watched the sheriff climbed up on his horse and started to ride away. Alex glanced at Tom and then back to the sheriff. The sheriff was riding up a storm as he disappeared down the road that led to town.

"He really has taken a liking to you, Alex," Tom said.

Alex turned to Tom with a proud grin.

"I like him too, but we've barely even met," Alex said politely.

"That's long enough for him. He'll know if he can trust someone after just a few seconds of talking to them. You've made a friend, and he trusts you," Tom said reassuringly.

"I'm glad. I wasn't sure," said Alex. "Is he here much?"

"He spends a lot of time in and around town and doesn't get home too early these days," Tom said.

"Sounds like my father. He's always at the bank and never home," Alex said.

"Your father works at the bank?" Tom's ears perked up.

"Yes, he does. He's the bank manager," he said rather proudly. Then he looked down as he thought about the fight that he had with his father.

"Let's go see your room," said Tom. He had asked Alex about his father several times during the trip. He never said much about his father. He must have had a bad falling out with him, he thought.

Tom led Alex through the house. They came to the end of the hallway. Tom opened the door and looked back at Alex.

"That's your room," said Tom.

"Alex, why don't you settle in, you still don't look that good. Get some rest. I'm going to head into town for a bit. Are you hungry?" said Tom.

"I'm a bit hungry," Alex said.

"Well get something from the kitchen if you like," Tom said as he turned to leave.

Alex was feeling a little uneasy.

"Thanks, Tom," Alex managed to say.

Tom took a step back. He looked at Alex with a half-smile and then went out the door.

"I'll be back later," Tom yelled back at Alex.

"See you later," Alex said.

Alex watched Tom leave down the hall and stood still for a

moment. This place is great, Alex thought. It was a refuge to Alex. Outside there were chickens, cows, horses and a large vegetable garden.

Alex turned to look at his room. It was bigger than his room back home. The room wasn't nearly as well kept as his old room was, but it was clean. They must have a housekeeper come by every once in a while, he thought. The sheriff and Tom didn't seem like the type to be this neat, he thought. He reached into his pocket, and he pulled out a small picture. He put it on the table that was next to his bed. It was a picture of his mother. He looked over at the picture and thought that she must be looking out for him. He remembered how she always took care of him and felt blessed that perhaps she had helped him to find Tom and the sheriff. Alex remembered what Gertrude had told him many times. Someday you'll have to create a whole new life just for you. You will end up having to take care of yourself, make your own decisions, and become a responsible adult. He hadn't really thought much about it since he figured this day would never come. However, it was here already.

After a short nap, Alex made his way to the kitchen. He found some bread carefully tucked away in the cupboard. It was the best bread he'd ever tasted. He was so hungry. He went out on the front porch and sat for a long while. He thought about his family and wondered how he could have ended up here so far from them. He looked out onto the fields and noticed how beautiful the scenery was. He could see clear all the way to the town. The view in all directions revealed more beauty than he had ever laid his eyes upon. He'd grown up in the city surrounded by roads and homes for as far as the eye could see. Here he was in the middle of the wilderness, surrounded by trees and hills and peacefulness. He looked again towards the city and noticed thin wispy trails of smoke reaching towards the sky. As he moved his gaze down towards the road, he could see a figure of a man on horseback quickly approaching. It was Tom.

Alex ran towards the front gate and waved at Tom. Tom reached the gate, red-faced and excited.

"Come, let's go into town," Tom said, grinning. "Go get your horse!"

Alex needed little convincing.

"I'll be right back," Alex said as he ran to get his horse.

He climbed on his horse and raced out from the back of the house to join Tom.

"Don't forget where the house is. It's the first ranch straight along this road that leads from the town," Tom said.

"I won't forget," Alex said thrilled beyond anything he'd ever experienced. He felt invigorated and alive. He was beginning to realize that he'd led a very sheltered life in the city.

The trip to the town was much shorter than Alex had expected. Alex found that the hilly countryside had concealed most of the view of the city. Alex smelled burning wood as they neared the city. The day had been a little cooler, so it was normal to smell the thick aroma of wood burning fireplaces or outdoor fires. But this smelled different. When they entered the city, they found chaos. People were running back and forth with pails of water to a building that was on fire. They stopped a couple of hundred feet from the burning building.

"Alex, let's tie up the horses over there," Tom said as he pointed to a hitching post next to the building with a sign that said, SHERIFF.

They quickly secured the horses and ran towards the fire. In the commotion, Alex lost sight of Tom. Alex ran straight into the middle of the chaos and joined in the battle to save the burning structure. Everything was going so fast, and he felt exhilarated. He ran to get buckets of water and pass them off to the train of people fighting the fire. He had noticed a beautiful young woman who seemed determined to get the fire put out.

"Get that water over there!" she yelled at Alex.

He saw her a few more times and then, once the fire was subdued, he lost sight of her. She was the most beautiful woman that he'd ever seen. He was looking around asking about her when Tom yanked at his arm.

"Alex! Where have you been?" Tom asked.

"Helping to get the fire put out," Alex said.

Alex looked over at Tom. He didn't have any ash on him. He didn't seem to even have much sweat on him.

"These town folk had it under control. Besides, there's a spanking new hotel opening up next week," Tom said.

Tom pointed towards a much larger building right next to what was left of the old hotel. Alex looked at the new building and then back to the smoldering ashes of the old hotel. Thick smoke had replaced the flames of the fire.

"It's a good thing that there was a pond close by. It sure did make it a lot easier to put out that fire," Alex said.

"Sure thing," Tom said with a bit of a grin on his face.

"Tom, I saw a young woman about our age that was barking orders to anyone who was filling the pails with water. Do you know who she is?" Alex asked.

"I don't rightly know who that might be," he lied. Her name was Jane, he thought to himself. She didn't care much for Tom. She had no hesitation in telling him so. He wouldn't give up on her, though.

"Why don't we head back home? It is getting late, and you're not so familiar with these roads at night. We still have a little bit of light left," Tom said.

They got home, put the horses away for the night and got cleaned up. It had been a long day for both of them. Tom disappeared into one of the other rooms and shut the door behind him. Alex stood there for a moment recounting the excitement of the day. He made his way to his room, found his bed and laid down. "What a day!" he said softly to himself. He closed his eyes, and before he could think another thought, he fell fast asleep.

18

Alex woke up to the sounds of gunshots. He looked out the window and saw Tom and the sheriff shooting at various objects sitting atop tree stumps. He watched them for a while from his window. Alex had a talent for learning through watching others. He imagined what it might be like to target practice with them. He pretended that he had a gun, took aim, and pulled the trigger.
"I think that I can do that," said Alex.
He dressed quickly and rushed to join them.

"Son, did you sleep well?" the sheriff asked.

"Yes, Sir! That's the best sleep that I've had in a long time," Alex said excitedly.

"Well son, how is your shooting?"

"I've never shot a gun before," Alex said. He was embarrassed to admit it.

"Come over here," said the sheriff with a proud smile. He really was thrilled to teach Alex how to shoot a gun. He thought about how much he missed having a son. That is why he liked having Tom around.

Alex came over, took the gun after some direction from the sheriff and tried his first shot. He hit the target dead on.

"That is great shooting! I thought you'd never shot a gun before," said the sheriff. He was suspicious.

"Sir, I've never shot a gun before. I'm a quick learner. I've been watching you and Tom shoot for a while," Alex said.

The sheriff put down his rifle and looked suspiciously at Alex. The sheriff didn't like the idea that Alex was "watching" him. "Well son, that was some good shooting. Why don't you and Tom go practice some more," he said. "Tom, go get Alex that gun that belonged to your father. I've got to go into town now."

The sheriff got onto his horse and rode to the gate. He turned and saw Alex and Tom still talking in the field. "He'll be a good companion for Tom," he muttered and then continued on his way to town.

Alex watched as the sheriff road away.

"Let's go get that gun," said Tom.

The two of them decided to eat something before going back out to do some more target practice. They fired a few more shots and then decided to go fishing.

"The fishing hole is up the road behind the house. It's not too far," Tom said.

"I love fishing," Alex said. He used to go fishing with his father when he was a young boy.

Alex and Tom got some worms and a homemade pair of fishing poles and made their way to the fishing hole. They had walked a ways before Tom asked, "Why did you run away from your home?"

Alex was surprised.

"I fought with my father the night that we were drinking in that barn," Alex said quickly.

"Are you going to go back?" Tom wanted to push Alex a little. They talked so much during the trip here, but Alex was tight-lipped about why he had left.

Alex hesitated for a little bit.

"No, I can't go back. I won't go back!" said Alexander raising his voice.

"Okay!" Tom said. "I just wanted to know if you were going to be around long enough to be my best friend."

Alex turned to Tom and smiled. "I've never had a best friend before."

"Well, you've got one now," Tom said triumphantly.

Alex thought for a second. He'd barely been gone a couple of days, and everything was so different here. He felt like he'd been in a long slumber for so many years now and finally he'd awakened.

After only a couple of days, he'd met the sheriff, made a new friend, had a nice gun that he was good at handling, and had met a girl while helping to put out a fire. He'd lived more life in the last two days than he had in his entire lifetime.

"Tom, I'm never going back home. This is paradise!" Alex said smiling.

They talked about growing up, finding their true loves, and having lots of fun. Neither one of them had had a close friend before. Tom was a bit less educated than Alex was. Alex found that he had been a bit too sheltered from life as he grew up.

Alex and Tom fished for an hour or so, before jumping in the river for a bit of fun. They romped about in the water, laughing and clowning around like two young schoolchildren. It occurred to Alex that this felt to him like a baptism of sorts. Perhaps this is the beginning of a new life for him. Memories of his own family were fading away from his thoughts bit-by-bit.

19

Alex had been living with the sheriff for two years now and was happy. Alex admired and respected the sheriff. The sheriff was gone all day and didn't get home until late at night. He would stop at the saloon on his way home and arrive home quite drunk. Alex found himself talking for quite a while with the drunken sheriff. Alex thought that the sheriff was actually a sagacious man. Alex thought that the sheriff was not quite as educated as a man his age should be. Sometimes the sheriff would fall asleep practically in mid-sentence. Ever since that night when he and the other boys sat in that old man's barn drinking whiskey, Alex couldn't stand the smell of whiskey. It made him nauseous. In spite of that, he really did enjoy the long talks that he had with the sheriff.

Afterward, Alex would go to his room and think about his life and where he was going with it. He had always wanted to make something of his life, and he didn't think that this was quite what he had in mind. Tom spent weeks at a time at his home in the big city with his mother. Alex often felt tempted to go down there with him and maybe visit with his family, but either Tom or the sheriff would convince him that it was not a very good idea. Alex had received a letter from his father asking him to come back home. He'd destroyed the letter and wrote back to his father to respect his privacy. He never told Tom or the sheriff about the letter.

When Tom came back into town, they would both carouse about town: go fishing, hunting, and all sorts of things. Alex had a splendid time. One day Tom was enjoying the company of a couple of women passing through town.

"Alex, come and join us?" Tom slurred his words together. "There is one for you and one for me," Tom said pointing to his two women companions. The two women were giggling and laughing.

"I gotta go feed the chickens," Alex said as he nearly ran to the door.

He could hear Tom yelling out after him as he walked out of the saloon. The saloon was crowded, so it wasn't obvious to anyone that Alex was cowardly retreating from an awkward situation. He walked briskly towards his horse.

"Hey, where are you off to in such a hurry?" Alex heard a woman say from somewhere behind him. He turned around and there standing next to him was that beautiful woman that he had met a couple of years ago. She was the one who had been barking orders at him while putting out the hotel fire.

"Hello," he somehow managed to say. His face went bright red. He'd thought about this woman, but never considered that he might meet her again.

"Well, Cowboy why don't you stay a while and talk with me," she said in a matter-of-fact tone with a beautiful smile.

"Of course, ma'am," Alex said as politely as he could. The last time someone called him a cowboy was when he was just a child. His father had called him a "little" cowboy.

"Ma'am? You're not talking to my mamma. My name is Jane. What's your name?" she said, laughing.

"My name is Alex. Pleased to meet you," he said. He was starting to relax a bit.

"Why don't we go sit by the hotel? It's too noisy over here," said Jane.

They walked over to the bench outside of the hotel and sat down.

"I saw you go into the saloon with Tom a little while ago, and I thought that you looked familiar," she said.

"You know Tom? I'm staying at his uncle's house," Alex said.

"Yes, I know Tom. We use to be friends a while back. We don't see eye-to-eye any longer," she said.

"Well, that's a shame. Tom is my best friend," Alex said.

"I never forget a face, and you sure do look familiar. Have you been here long?" Jane said as she looked him over.

"We met the night of the hotel fire a couple of years ago. You were dishing out orders to fill the pails with water and get them moving up the line. There was so much chaos that night. And that was the day I arrived into town," he said as he remembered how beautiful and forceful he found her to be that night.

"I remember you now. I don't remember why, but when I saw you that evening, I suddenly felt that everything was going to be okay. And, it was. We were able to put that fire out and prevent it from engulfing the adjacent buildings. We were going to tear it down anyway. The sheriff said that it looked like a dog had overturned a lamp in the study, but it sure did look suspicious. I suppose it doesn't really matter much now. The new hotel is bigger and better than the old one," she said.

"This is a beautiful hotel. I don't come into town too often. When I do, I can't help but admire it. I spend most of my time around the sheriff's ranch, tending to my duties there. Do you live around here?" Alex asked.

Jane pointed in the opposite direction of the sheriff's house. "I live in that direction. I don't come into town too often. But when I do, I stay in my daddy's hotel. I love it here."

"You must be very proud of him," Alex smiled.

"I-" Jane stopped. She recognized Tom's voice. She and Alex turned to see the disruption that was coming from the saloon. They saw Tom staggering towards them.

"So there you are, Alex, with my girl!" Tom slurred.

"Tom, you drunken fool. I never have been and never will be any such thing to you. My Papa warned you to keep your distance from me. Besides your two girls are waiting for you over there," she pointed toward the saloon. Two women were walking towards Tom.

"Alex, why don't you come back in? The girls have been asking for you," Tom insisted.

He wasn't slurring his words anymore. He was angry.

"Tom, I'll be over a little later," Alex yelled.

Jane stood up.

"I have to go. My father is expecting me," Jane said. She knew that Tom was angry, and he was drunk.

Alex stood.

Jane knew Tom all too well. The adrenaline was pumping through his veins, negating the effects of the alcohol. She knew that Tom could snap in an instant and release a torrent of irrational hostility. She was the only one that noticed that Tom had placed his right hand on his gun that was nestled in his holster.

"Oh, all right Jane. You can have him. He's my best friend anyhow," Tom said. His slur had returned. He turned back towards the saloon and waved with his empty right hand while the two women giggled and laughed with him all the way back into the saloon.

Alex turned to Jane.

"Jane, I'm sorry about that," Alex said. "He's had too much to drink."

"I really do have to get going. Why don't you come back on Saturday morning around ten? We can spend the day together and have a nice little picnic," she said with a broad smile.

"That would be wonderful. I'll be here on Saturday," he said as she disappeared into the hotel.

Alex could hardly contain his excitement. He thought about going into the saloon and talking with Tom, but he knew that Tom was too drunk. Alex was annoyed with him for interrupting his visit with Jane. Alex decided that he would talk with him in the morning. Alex rode home as fast as he'd ever ridden. He was thrilled that he had met the woman of his dreams. He would often daydream about her and had hoped that someday he might meet her again. He led his horse to the barn and gave him some food. It had been a very long day for Alex, so he just went to bed and fell into a deep slumber.

The morning light nudged him awake from his calm, relaxing sleep. He jumped out of bed, cleaned himself up, ate, and called out for Tom. No one answered. No matter, he thought. He ran outside, fed the chickens, the pigs and set about to feed the horses. He looked over and saw that Tom's horse was gone. Odd, he thought. No matter how drunk he is, Tom always comes home. Just then, the sheriff walked up from behind him.

"Did you and Tom have a fight or something? Tom saddled up his horse this morning and told me he'd be back in a couple of weeks. He said that he didn't want to be around you for a little while," the sheriff asked.

"No, sir. Tom's my best friend. Last night he had a little too much to drink. He saw me talking to this girl Jane. He said that she was his girl. Jane denied it. Anyhow, after a while he seemed to change his mind and left us alone," Alex said innocently.

"Oh hell! He fell for her a long time ago. He can't get it through his thick skull that they ain't right for each other. Son, give him a little time. Dangit, he has all these women hanging all over him, and he can't just let this one go. I'm headed into town. I'll see you later," the sheriff said.

"Goodbye," said Alex relieved.

Alex spent the day doing chores around the ranch. He had a spring in his step and found himself whistling the day away.

20

Still no Tom, Alex thought as he rode into town. It was a bright, beautiful Saturday morning when he left to meet Jane. He'd never gone on a date before. He felt like he'd met the woman of his dreams. He arrived a few minutes early. No matter, he thought. He didn't mind waiting. As he turned the corner, the hotel entrance came into full view. There, just right of the front door, he saw Jane seated on the bench. She was a remarkable sight.

"Hi there!" she said with the most beautiful smile he'd ever seen.

"Hello Jane," he said as he got down from his horse. "I thought I was early."

"I was even earlier," she said as she laughed.

Alex smiled. Now he knew that Jane had a competitive streak in her.

"I thought that we'd walk over to the park and have a nice picnic. I know a beautiful spot. First, come meet my father. He wants to meet you. He's just inside," she said.

"Your father?" he asked hesitantly.

She took him by the hand and led him inside. A group of men stood talking and laughing with each other in the far corner of the room.

Jane motioned to her father to come over.

"Excuse me, gentlemen, I'll be right back," her father said to the other men as he walked over to join his daughter. He was a short, stout man with glasses and a well-trimmed mustache.

"You must be Alex. My daughter has been talking about you incessantly all morning," he said as he glanced at his daughter.

Jane blushed.

"It's nice to meet you," Alex said as he shook hands with him.

"You have a good, firm handshake. I can tell a lot about a man by his handshake. I can see you are a well-mannered gentleman. I trust that you will take good care of my daughter," he said as he looked squarely into Alex's eyes.

"Yes sir, of course," Alex quickly said.

Jane rested her hand on Alex's arm.

"Oh, Papa! We are going to have a picnic in the park. If you need me, I'll be over there," Jane said as she pointed to the lovely park just a few yards away from the hotel.

"Alright, daughter, have a great time," he glanced approvingly to Alex with a nod.

"Goodbye sir," Alex said as he opened the door for Jane.

Jane picked up a picnic basket that was next to the door.

"Let me get that," he took the basket, and they strolled leisurely to the park.

They chose a clearing under a tree with a beautiful view of the lake. Jane pulled out a large blanket and carefully laid it out. She placed the basket on one corner and began to set out what seemed to Alex to be a mouth-watering, savory feast of bread, chicken, some kind of desserts and much more.

"This looks so delicious," Alex said.

"I hope that you like it," she said.

They spent the next hour eating and getting to know each other.

"I feel like I've known you all of my life," she said.

"I feel the same way about you. It was great to meet your father. Is your mother at the hotel?" he asked.

"She was there. She helped me put the picnic basket together. She left early this morning with my aunt. They were headed back home. I'll head home with my father later today," she said. "Where is your mother?"

"She died a while back when I was a young one," he moved uncomfortably.

"I'm sorry," she said as she quickly changed the subject. "Let's go for a walk by the water. It is so beautiful today. And I feel so lucky to have met you ... again," she said.

They talked about all sorts of things for the next few hours. Alex told Jane about his mother and that he still missed her very much. He told her all about the fight that he had with his father and how much he missed Greta, his brother, and his sister. No matter, though, he told her, he was happy that he was living with the sheriff and Tom.

"Why wouldn't you want to see your family again?" she asked innocently. She loved her parents dearly, and could not imagine life without them.

"Maybe someday..." he said while drifting off in thought. He remembered about the letter that he'd received from his father and that he'd told his father never to write again. He never received another letter from his father.

"Now that I've met you, I'll never leave you," he said and then quickly caught himself. "I mean..." Alex said.

"Alex, you are the kindest, most considerate and loving person that I've ever met. I'll never leave you either," she said affectionately.

"Let's get home. If you like, I'll be back next Saturday," she said as a faint blush reddened her cheeks.

"I'll call on you at 10 AM. Perhaps you'd like to go riding in the hills on the far side of the lake?" he said.

"I love to ride. Yes, that sounds fantastic!"

They continued to meet every Saturday over the next year. Sometimes they'd go riding, other times picnic and a few times they even went swimming with her family and friends. As time passed, they became closer and closer. Jane's mother had taken a liking to Alex. At first, Alex was a little uncomfortable coming over to Jane's house to join them for supper. He got over that quickly. He was falling in love with Jane. He found he had a deep affection for her parents too.

During the week, Alex would often come to town to help Jane's father with chores around the hotel. Even his best friend Tom was happy for him. Alex thought back to just a year ago, he and Tom's friendship had seemed to hit a snag. Tom had distanced himself a bit from Alex by spending more time at his mother's house. Tom had some friends there that he enjoyed carousing around with, so it wasn't hard for him to keep his distance from Alex. Tom quickly forgot about any bad blood between him and his best friend when he fell in love with a beautiful girl that lived just a few doors down from his mother's house. Alex noticed that Tom was a changed man. Although not as often as before, Tom and Alex would still hunt and ride together. Occasionally Tom and his girl would join Alex and Jane for a picnic together.

Two more years passed during which they would all have a very good time. Alex was thrilled to spend time with Tom, his best friend, and Jane, the love of his life. Alex had been courting Jane for three years, and he felt it was time for him to propose marriage to her.

Jane told him that she would marry him the following year.

21

Alex was grateful to the sheriff. He felt indebted to him. The sheriff had welcomed him into his home nearly six years ago. Alex had found a purposeful life. During that time, he became proficient at riding. He was an expert shooter both with the pistol that the sheriff gave him as well as the rifle that Tom had given him.

"I'm very proud of you, Alex," the sheriff said.

"Thank you, Sir. You've been really kind to me all these years. I owe you a debt of gratitude. I hope I can repay you someday," said Alex with a confidence he had never felt before.

"Son, I'm looking for a deputy to help me out. You really know how to handle that pistol I gave you. And you're not too bad on that horse either," the sheriff said. He knew that Alex would want to settle down soon and would need a steady source of income.

"Thank you, sir," Alex said proudly. "I'd appreciate that very much. But, Jane and I will be getting married soon, and we've talked about moving to San Francisco."

The sheriff winced. The sheriff did not like his offers turned down.

"Have you seen Tom?" asked the sheriff.

"No, sir. Tom said he would be back tomorrow."

Tom was still living in San Francisco with his mother, and he would head back to the small town where his uncle lived every few weeks and stay with his uncle for a few days each time. When Tom was back in town, he and Alex would go carousing about the town. Alex would never drink, though. However, Tom would get drunk almost as bad as his uncle.

"Well son, think about it anyway. You never know what the future might bring," the sheriff insisted.

Alex nodded. He felt a little odd hearing those words from the sheriff. They seemed oddly familiar and full of wisdom. He thought that Greta would have said something like that.

Tom came back the next day right before sunset.

"Tom, welcome back!" Alex said with an edge of excitement. Alex was sitting on the porch when he saw Tom ride up.

Tom got down from his horse. He led his horse to the hitching post next to the porch.

"Alex, do you know someone named Marcus?" Tom asked even though he already knew the answer.

Alex's face paled as his brows tightened. He hadn't heard that name in quite a while. He didn't think much about his "old" family anymore. It hurt too much to think about them. He was happy with his new family.

"That is my brother's name," Alex said.

"He told me that he'd been looking for his brother for quite some time," said Tom.

"What did you tell him?" Alex asked.

"I told him about you, how we met, and that we rode up here a few years ago. I told him about my uncle and that you live here. He said that his father worked for the bank. After we had talked for a while, he was convinced that you're his brother."

Alex felt his past coming back to his present with a vengeance. He had done his best to repress memories of that life that he left behind so long ago. He had preferred to forget those painful memories. He had a new life now with people who cared for him. He had a wonderful relationship with Jane. After three years of courting, they had decided to marry. How would he mesh this life of freedom, responsibility, and independence with that old one of immaturity, mistakes, Gertrude,

Marissa, Marcus, and his father? Then he thought about Jane. She wanted to move to San Francisco.

"Where's the sheriff?" Tom asked Alex. Alex didn't seem to hear him.

"Where is my uncle?" Tom yelled.

Alex snapped out of his fog.

"He's inside," said Alex.

Tom ran up the steps and disappeared into the house. Alex felt alone for the first time in a very long time. Alex went for a ride. He had to think.

Tom told the sheriff all about Alex's father and brother. He said that Alex's father was the manager of a bank in San Francisco.

The sheriff listened intently.

"So his father works at the bank. Perhaps we should meet him," the sheriff said.

Back in San Francisco, Marcus burst into the parlor with so much enthusiasm that it startled Marissa and Gertrude, who were sitting by the window mending some clothes.

"You'll never guess what happened," he said with barely a breath left in him. "I've found Alex!"

"Calm down, boy! Why don't you sit over here for a moment and tell us slowly what happened," Gertrude said as she set the clothes aside.

He sat down on the creaky wooden chair next to Gertrude. He looked over at Marissa and noticed that her eyes had become darker and intense. He had learned long ago to always listen to Marissa when her mood would change in this manner. He was about to ask Marissa what was wrong, but Gertrude said, "Now out with it!"

Marissa's eyes intensified as she calmly said. "Where is he?"

"I was talking to this man while I was out riding on the south side of town, his name is Tom, I think. Anyhow, we talked about a few things and then I told him that I often ride in the hopes of someday finding my brother. He asked me what he looked like. I described Alex to him, and the man knew instantly that I was talking about Alex,"

Marcus said with barely a breath between his words.

Marissa's eyes began to transform into those of joy, "Did Tom tell you where Alex is?"

Marcus paused, still a little out of breath.

"Well, Marcus, tell us!" Gertrude said.

"Yes!" Marcus shouted with all his might.

Just then, his father entered the parlor.

"What is all this ruckus about?" Alexander said teasingly.

"I found Alex!" Marcus exclaimed again.

The color quickly left Alexander's face. His face went to staunch disbelief as he stepped back nearly losing his balance. He never told them that he had found Alex some time before. That was when Alex had written him to stay away.

"Where is he?" he said softly.

"He's in a small town not too far from here. He lives with the sheriff of that town. Isn't this great, Father? We can be a family again," Marcus said.

"We must..." Alexander started.

Gertrude shot a look across to Alexander.

"Supper is almost ready. We can discuss this after dinner!" she said sternly. She was worried that Alexander might need some time to recover from this incredible, but shocking news.

Alexander paused for a moment and then spoke, "Let's get ready for supper."

During supper, Marissa and Marcus were talking about how wonderful it would be to have Alex back at the dinner table.

"I wonder if he has a beard," Marcus said.

"Marcus, how silly is that?" Marissa shot back. She giggled.

"Well, then maybe he has a mustache," Marcus said.

"Nope, no mustache either," Marissa said in her usual matter of fact way. "I miss him."

"I do too!" Marcus said.

The banter went back and forth between Marcus and Marissa with an occasional word from Gertrude. Alexander never said a word.

After supper, Alexander went out on the porch and thought about Alex. Alexander thought about how determined he'd been to find his son. However, after he had found him, Alex had made it very clear that he did not want to come home. Alexander was hurt but decided to honor his son's request. Alexander had kept this news from his family because he was certain that it would hurt them. He felt a little better to write letters to his prodigal son. He had never sent them. He was determined to preserve the integrity of his family and found this practice helped lessen the pain of losing his son. Alexander took a deep breath and then let it out slowly. He heard footsteps coming towards the front door. He looked towards the door and saw Gertrude peering at him through the doorway.

Gertrude walked out of the house and sat next to him. "Alexander, you know that you have to meet with him. Perhaps you could convince him to come home just for a little visit."

"Gertrude, I've always listened to your sound advice, but Alex abandoned us. He left his family. He's been gone for such a long time. Why would he want to come back now?" Alexander said.

"Alexander, listen to me. I know that your son loves you. It's just that the both of you are so stubborn, neither one of you would ever think of making a move. One of you has to just take that first step," Gertrude said with the voice of wisdom and reason. "This couldn't have been easy for him either. It's been hard for all of us."

"I know that you are right. I've missed Alex every day that he's been gone. I would give anything if he were here right now. I do love my son. There is a heaviness in my heart that I cannot explain any other way. There is a bank coach headed that way in the morning. I'll be on it."

Gertrude got up and turned back to Alexander, "May God be with you on your journey," she said as she turned and reached for the door. Marissa was standing in the doorway.

"Father, please wait one more day before you go. I have a dreadful feeling," Marissa said with wisdom way beyond her years.

"Don't worry, dearest Marissa. Everything will be okay. Now get ready for bed," Alexander said.

Gertrude took Marissa by the hand and led her back to her room. They left Alexander alone on the porch.

Alexander sat there on the porch thinking and started to cry tears of joy.

22

Alexander left the house early before the children woke up. His bank made regular trips to many of the surrounding towns. He went to the bank where he worked and picked up a small sum of money from his account. He was a little early, so he sat on the bench outside the entrance and waited for the coach. He thought about what he would say to his son. He missed him more than he had realized. He wiped an errant tear from his eye before it had a chance to reveal his thoughts and feelings to anyone that might be passing by.

He heard the coach approach and gathered his belongings. It pulled up just a few feet from him. He looked at his pocket watch and saw that it was on time. He hurriedly entered the coach and waited for its cargo to be loaded. It seemed to him that time was moving slower than usual. The ride to the small town where his son now lived was uneventful. He had fallen asleep shortly after leaving the city. He was pleasantly surprised to hear the driver announce that they were approaching the town. Shortly after arriving, he found boarding at the local hotel. He did not want to waste too much time, so he got cleaned up and went in search of his son. He had asked the hotel clerk where to find the sheriff's office. The hotel patron laughed and said, "The sheriff's office is right across the street; though you'd do better if you looked for him in the saloon first!"

Alexander was walking in the direction of the sheriff's office when something caught his eye in the alley next to the adjoining building. It appeared to be near the back door of the saloon. A man was brandishing his pistol yelling and laughing at the same time.

"Now Howard, come on back," said the other man in the alley.

"Nobody cares about my troubles," said the man with the pistol. He was very drunk and could barely stand without falling.

"We all care about you. It's just that you talk too much sometimes. I've told you to watch what you say."

The drunken man fell flat on his face and just closed his eyes. It looked like he just passed out.

Alexander approached them cautiously.

"Is he alright?" asked Alexander.

The sheriff looked up as if caught by surprise.

"Yes, he'll be okay. He's just been drinking more than he should," said the sheriff.

"Tom, get out here and take care of Mr. Jackson," the sheriff yelled into the saloon. A few seconds later Tom came out of the saloon.

Could this be the same Tom that Marcus talked about? Alexander thought as he shot a quick glance at Tom.

"Let's go in and get a drink, Mr. Jackson," said Tom.

"What brings you to our fine town?" said the sheriff to Alexander as he led him quickly into the back entrance of the saloon.

"My name is Alexander Johnson. I am here on bank business in your fine town," said Alexander.

The sheriff hesitated. The name sounded oddly familiar to him, he thought.

"My name is Sheriff Thomas Jefferson Buchanan. Everyone just calls me Sheriff. You work for the bank?" said the sheriff rather intently.

"Yes, I am a bank manager. I am also here to find my son. I understand that you know him. His name is Alex."

"How would you know this?" asked the sheriff suspiciously.

"My younger son met your nephew a couple of days ago back in San Francisco," said Alexander.

"And why do you want to talk to him. He has been here for years. He has never mentioned anything about a father in all this time," said the sheriff. This was not true. Alex talked quite a bit about his father with the sheriff during those evenings when the drunken sheriff and Alex would chat. The sheriff had learned all about Alex's father.

The sheriff would never dole out information to a stranger. The sheriff knew that Alex had actually wanted to see his father but had convinced Alex that it would not be a good idea. He told Alex that if Alex's father really wanted, he'd have come for him a long time ago. Alex trusted the sheriff.

"Sir, I realize how this must seem to you. I have not rested since my son and I had parted ways. He is my reason for living. It was never my desire to drive my son away. Moreover, it is not my intention to take him away from his life here either. I ask only to speak with him," said Alexander.

"Father?" said Alex. He had heard part of the conversation between his father and the sheriff.

Alexander turned around and saw his son standing in the doorway to the saloon.

"Son! How are you?" said Alexander as he ran to greet his son.

The sheriff narrowed his eyes.

"I'll leave you two alone. I need to take care of some business. Alex, let me know if you need me," said the sheriff.

Alexander reached for his son's arm. Alex stepped back.

"Son, I'm sorry. I'm sorry for everything. We've all missed you so."

"Why did you come here?" Alex asked suspiciously.

"I've come to make peace with you and to ask you to return home, just for a visit. We all miss you very much."

"I have a life here, now. I can't just up and leave," Alex said. Then he realized that that is exactly what he had done when he left home.

"I understand," said Alexander as he cleared his throat. "What have you been doing all this time?"

Alexander wanted to be very careful to exercise his patience and understanding, as a father should. Gertrude had told him to set his expectations aside and just be his father.

Alex's mood softened. He really was excited to see his father. He'd told Jane that he had decided to contact his father to see if they could patch up their relationship.

"I've become quite the expert at riding, roping, and handling my pistol," Alex said proudly. He was excited to see his father. He wished that things had been different.

"I'd really like to see you do that sometime!" Alexander said proudly.

Alex smiled broadly.

"Have you eaten yet?" said Alex.

"Not yet. I'm so hungry!" Alexander said. He was glad that he and his son were talking. Alexander was warmly surprised at how his son had grown into a solidly mature man. Alex seemed a bit more rugged as if life had not been very kind to him.

They got something to eat and talked for a long time. They talked about life here in this little town, about Alex's adventures, about life back at home with Marcus, Marissa, and Gertrude. They talked about everything. They were both laughing and having a great time. Alexander pulled out his pocket watch and sighed.

"I need to go to the bank to take care of some business. But before I go, here is something for you," said Alexander. Alexander handed Alex a pouch containing some money, a pocket watch, and an assortment of small gold nuggets.

"This is for you son. I wanted you to know that I do love you very much. I know that it's been very hard for you for a very long time. I'm sorry that I was not there for you when you needed me. I want you to know that I'm here for you now," said Alexander.

"I understand, Father," he said. Alex looked through the pouch at the various items. He found a small cross that looked vaguely familiar.

"That was your mother's favorite. She wore it always. When you were a young boy, you would ask incessantly for it. She told you that when you were older, she would give it to you. She made me promise that I gave it to you when the time was right."

Alex's eyes began to well up. He looked away for a bit to regain his composure.

"I remember," said Alex.

"Alex, I leave on the morning coach back to San Francisco. There's room in the coach if you'd want to ride back home. You could take the coach back here next week."

"I'll think about it, Father. Like I said, I have responsibilities here now."

"I understand son. You are welcome home anytime."

This time, Alexander's eyes welled up. He did not attempt to conceal his tears. Instead, he rose up, embraced his son and said, "I'm so proud of you, Son."

Alex rode back to the place he'd called home for the last few years. He was so incredibly happy. He felt like a huge weight had lifted off his shoulders. He rode like the wind. He wanted to tell the sheriff that he was going to be gone for a little while. He knew that the sheriff would understand.

No one was home when he got there. That was odd, he thought. The sheriff had left the saloon before he did. He went to bed and got up early. Still no sheriff. He left a note:

> "I'm headed to the stagecoach with my father. The coach leaves at 8 AM to deliver a bank shipment. I'll be back in a few days."

He gathered enough clothes for a short trip and rode his horse to join his father at the hotel.

23

Alexander bolted up from his deep sleep. He was choking and gasping for air. He was grasping at his neck trying to free himself from the bed linens that had somehow wrapped around his neck. He calmed himself down and realized that it was just a dream.

"Some dream! It was more like a nightmare," he muttered, his voice raspy. He rubbed his neck and cleared his throat. It was as if he had slept for days. He felt nauseous.

His thoughts were scattered and unfocused.

"What is wrong with me? Did I drink that much?"

He sat up and looked around. He saw a jumble of shapes and colors accompanied with a chaotic jumble of noises that lacked any sense. He tried to stand, steadying himself on the table next to his bed and then quickly sat back down. He closed his eyes for several minutes until his nausea began to recede. He laid down and closed his eyes. He felt calm returning to him as he fell back into a deep sleep.

"Wake up. Wake up," said a voice.

Alexander began to stir.

"Wake up! Wake up!" said the voice again much louder this time.

Alexander strained to open his eyes. Alex was standing next to the bed.

"Get up, Father," said Alex.

"What?" asked Alexander.

He was still disoriented, but feeling much better.

"You need to get ready," said Alex.

"Get ready for what," said Alexander.

"Get ready to go home," said Alex.

"Go home?" Alexander said.

"You need to get yourself together," said Alex.

Alexander was still confused. He began to sit up. Things seemed odd to him, but he couldn't put his finger on exactly what it was.

"What is going on?" Alexander asked.

"I'm here to go home with you. It's time to go home," said Alex.

Alexander slowly got up.

"I did not sleep very well," Alexander said with a raspy voice.

Alexander cleared his throat and looked up at Alex.

"So you decided to come home," Alexander said. "Marissa, Marcus, and Gertrude will be very happy to see you."

"Of course, Father. I am looking forward to seeing them too. You know that I can't stay there very long," said Alex.

"I understand, Alex," Alexander said half-heartedly.

"Father, do you need help gathering your things?" Alex said as he looked around and saw a satchel sitting on the chair, a pair of boots, and a picture of a small child on the floor next to the bed.

"No. I did not bring much with me," Alexander said.

Alex went over to the picture and picked it up.

"Who is the child that is in this picture?" said Alex thinking that it might be him.

"That is a picture of you when you were four years old. See the barn in the background. If you look just to the right of the barn, you can see your mother. She was always nearby. That picture is my favorite. I've always traveled with it. And when I'm not traveling, I keep it on my desk at work," Alexander said endearingly.

"I don't remember," Alex said with a twinge of pain.

"I have some more pictures at home. You may have that one if you would like," Alexander said.

Alexander walked over to the table behind Alex, and picked up a few other things and put them into his satchel. He sat back down on the bed and put his boots on. He looked across the room, near the door and noticed a small bundle.

"What is that bundle by the door?" said Alexander.

"It is some clothes and a few things I thought I might need," Alex answered.

Alexander smiled.

Alexander reached for his coat, his satchel, and a pocket watch that was on the table nearest to the window.

"Well, this is all that I have, and I'm ready to go," Alexander said.

"Father, I can only leave here for just a few days. I have responsibilities here, I would be remiss to forego them," Alex said apologetically.

"I understand, Alex. I am very proud of you. I am glad that you are returning with me today," Alexander said cheerfully.

The conversation between them was not easy. Each had much more to say to the other than they could manage. Alexander wanted to tell his son that he loved him more than life itself. Alex wanted to tell his Father that he always loved and respected him and that he thought about him each day.

Alexander walked to the door and opened it.

"Let's go?" Alexander said, smiling.

The door opened to a long hallway with a banister on the left and more rooms on the right. The stairs were about twenty-five feet in front of them. One set of stairs led up to the third floor, and the second set of stairs led down to the street level.

"Okay," answered Alex.

Alexander started to walk across the narrow hallway. As he approached the stairway, he looked up and hesitated. He saw the stairs that were leading up and froze. A wave of nausea hit him like a ton of bricks. Alex was right behind him and was not able to stop so quickly. Alexander lost his balance as Alex collided with Alexander's satchel. Alexander tripped as the satchel wedged between his legs and fell.

"Father, what's wrong?" Alex said confused.

The glaze lifted from Alexander's eyes.

"I'm sorry son, I don't know what happened," Alexander said, still a little dazed.

"That's okay, Father," said Alex.

Alex helped his father get up and led the way down the stairs. Alexander followed behind and stopped at the counter.

"Son, go ahead. I'll take care of business downstairs and meet you outside," said Alexander.

He watched Alex walk out the front door. Through the large picture window, he saw his son sit down on the bench right outside the door. He smiled and then turned to the clerk and handed him some money.

He picked up his bag and walked quickly to the door. It still had not sunken in completely that his son was coming home with him. He walked out the door and sat down next to his son as they both waited for the coach to arrive.

The day was unfolding to be bright and sunny as the sun continued to rise from its deep slumber. The hotel was located on a busy thoroughfare where many townspeople were walking about. None of them paid much attention to the father and son seated on the hotel porch bench. Alex leaned forward and looked down towards the floor. Then he looked over to where the old hotel once stood.

"Father, did you know that this hotel is six years old," said Alex.

"No, it's older than that, I stayed here eight or so years ago," Alexander said.

"Father, that hotel was destroyed in a fire," Alex said. "It was over there."

Alexander looked in the direction where Alex was pointing and then back at the door to the hotel.

"Oh. It's been a long time since I've been here. I guess it does look different."

Alexander looked back at Alex.

"Have you got any friends here?" said Alexander.

"Yes, I have a few friends. My best friend is Tom. We go hunting and fishing quite often...," He hesitated and took a deep breath. "But not lately. I've also met a young woman that I care for very much," Alex said as the edge of his lips curled upward.

"That's wonderful, Son. How did you meet her?" Alexander said smiling. He thought about when he met Martha, the love of his life.

"Actually, I first met her when we were putting out the hotel fire when I first came to town," he said rather proudly. "But I did not formally meet her until a couple of years later."

"Why did it take so long to meet, I mean the second time?" Alexander said. He remembered that he'd been courting his wife soon after meeting her.

"She lives on a ranch on the other side of town and neither one of us would come into town very often. I saw her a few times during those two years, but a respectable moment had not presented itself," Alex said as he sat up and smiled proudly.

"Son, I am so very proud of you. What are your intentions?" Alexander smiled back.

"I had a talk with her this morning. I told her that I was going home to visit my family. When I return, I told her that I planned to ask her father for her hand.

"What is she like?" Alexander said curiously. He had not expected this wonderful news. He was so proud of his son. He thought how he had never seen this side of him before.

"She is beautiful with her long brown hair. She is outspoken – that's for sure. She's very smart. She told me that she would like to go to a university to continue her education. I don't remember exactly what she wants to study, but it has something to do with business. That cannot happen here in this little town," Alex said. He was getting more comfortable as he spoke about Jane.

"Alex, Jane sounds like a lovely young woman. I would very much like to meet her parents someday, and of course, Jane too," Alexander said. He thought that the parents should always meet each other. It was only proper. Alexander thought for a moment what his wife might think about Jane and Alex. The words came quickly to his mind: "Mind your business, and let your son be! Alex is a grown man now!"

"They would very much like to meet you. I spoke with her parents about you too. They are very excited to meet you too. I told them that you are a banker and on occasion travel by coach to many different cities. They hoped that you would return soon," Alex's eyes were shining brightly as he spoke.

"I look forward to meeting them," he said. "It would be an honor to meet them. What line of business is Jane's father in?"

"He owns this hotel," said Alex.

"Is he here now?" said Alexander excitedly. He thought perhaps he could meet Jane's father right now.

"No. Jane's father does not come into town too often. He has a ranch about five miles east of here," said Alex. "Besides, the stagecoach should be arriving shortly."

Almost as if on cue, the stagecoach drawn by six beautiful horses approached the town square.

24

The horses seemed very animated in their movements. They displayed an air of nobility as they pulled the coach. The stagecoach made its way through the center of town and then went around the large pond. The same pond that had provided the water to put out the old hotel fire. The horses had made the trip many times and would have completed the turn without disaster, but the driver insisted that the horses slow down and keep their distance from that pond. He had heard about a coach that had gotten too close once before, and the coach and all of its occupants ended up in the middle of the pond though no one was seriously hurt. Once the coach had safely passed the pond, the driver steered the horses along the narrow trail leading to the hotel and noticed two men seated near the hotel entrance. He guided the horses very near to the front door of the hotel, and called, "Whoa!" The horses obliged and came to a dead stop. The coach driver hesitated for a moment before securing the coach. He climbed down from his perch.

"Are you gentlemen going to get on the coach or not?" said the stagecoach driver very impatiently.

Alex was the first to rise. He gave the bags to the driver and made his way to the coach. As Alex opened the door, he noticed that there were some people already seated in the coach. Alexander climbed into the coach. Alexander sat in the seat directly opposite two other passengers. Alex climbed in and took the seat next to his father.

"Hello, Mr. Johnson," said one of the passengers.

In unison, both father and son responded, "Hello."

Alexander looked over at his son and then to Charles and Victoria Adams. Alexander knew them, as they were loyal bank customers who frequented the bank where he worked.

"Hello, Charles. What a pleasant surprise to see you and your beautiful wife, Victoria. This is my son Alex," said Alexander.

"Hello, Ma'am. Hello, Sir," said Alex. He was not interested in chatting with Charles and Victoria. He wanted to talk with his father and to continue talking about his plans for the future. However, they seemed nice enough, and he felt that he could speak freely in front of them.

"Hello son," said Charles and Victoria.

Victoria looked over to Alexander and asked, "You don't look very well, Mr. Johnson, are you okay?"

"Yes, I'm all right," Alexander quickly responded. "Thank you for asking. You look beautiful as ever."

"Why, thank you! That is very kind of you to say," said Victoria.

"Alex and I are on our way home. Alex has been away for a while, and we are all excited for his visit," said Alexander.

A look of recognition flashed across Victoria's face along with a large smile. "Alex, yes, I do remember you. Aren't you the eldest son?"

"Yes, ma'am," said Alex. He was hoping that she would lose interest in conversing soon.

"It was a pleasure to see you both. I'll let you two alone. I'm sure you have plenty to talk about," said a perceptive Victoria.

Alex displayed a polite smile and nodded his head.

Alexander smiled at Victoria and then turned to Alex.

"Alex, please tell me more about Jane," Alexander said to his son. Alexander knew that Victoria could talk and talk. He was grateful that Victoria allowed them some privacy.

"Jane? Who's Jane?" asked Victoria.

Alexander took a deep breath and let it out all at once.

Charles looked up from his paper, "Darling, why don't you let them be."

Victoria looked disapprovingly at Charles and then sat back with her mouth closed tight.

Alex ignored Victoria's question and continued.

"Father, I care about Jane very much," said Alex.

Alexander looked over to his son, and paused for a moment, "Has she thought about what university that she would like to attend? Most of the universities are back east."

"We've talked about it quite a bit. Jane is very anxious to get on with the rest of her life. She wants to study something in business, just like you," he said hesitantly.

"Your mother also went to the university to learn her business skills," said Alexander.

Alexander and his son continued to talk about Jane for quite a while.

Victoria was a little annoyed. A twinge of compassion suggested to her that it might be better if she would retreat and allow these two a little bit of privacy. She murmured a soft sigh, got comfortable, and carefully placed her head on her husband's shoulder. Victoria drifted off to sleep. Several minutes had passed when the coach jostled about and brought Victoria out of her sleep. She looked up and saw that her husband had dozed off. She thought with all of this rocking and bumping it was a wonder that anyone could sleep. She looked over to Alexander and saw that he had his hat over his face and must be sleeping. His son seemed to be lost in thought as he looked out the window. Alex reminded her of her beloved husband during their courtship days.

"Alex," she whispered to Alex.

"Yes Ma'am," he responded hesitantly.

"Pardon me, but I could not help overhearing you and your father earlier," said Victoria hesitantly.

Alex looked up at her politely.

"I met my husband so many years ago and fell in love with him when I first met him. I love him with all of my heart. I can see that you feel the same way about your Jane," she said as a tear made its way down her cheek. She quickly drew her kerchief to wipe away her emotion.

"Thank you, Ma'am," he said uncomfortably. She had caught him completely off guard. He felt a wealth of warmth and caring wash over him. "I love Jane very much. When I'm with her, or even just thinking of her, I feel so happy," said Alex.

"I could see that while you were talking about her earlier. It makes me happy when I see young people falling in love. I know that the two of you will eventually be together. Your love will help each of you to find each other again…," she said as she looked intently into his eyes. Her eyes were full of wisdom and compassion.

"Thank you, Ma'am," he said.

"I better get some rest," she said. She smiled softly at Alex and then rested her head on her husband's shoulder and closed her eyes. Alex looked across to Mrs. Adams and smiled. He stretched his arms and moved in his seat. It was somewhat cramped in the coach. He was uncomfortable in this small claustrophobic enclosed space. He started to get a headache. He closed his eyes and tried to fall asleep to no avail.

"Father, are you awake?" he whispered to his father.

Alexander moved his hat up and looked at Alex.

"Father, tell me about my mother," said Alex.

"I loved your mother very much," Alexander started.

Alex shifted uncomfortably in his seat and asked, "Why did you let her die?"

Alex looked at the floor of the cab then at his father and then back down to the floor.

Alexander looked affectionately at his son and paused for a long time before he spoke.

"Son, I loved your mother very much. Your mother was a lovely woman. She loved you with all of her heart. I remember when you were born. When I came in to see you that beautiful day, she was already holding you, and crying with joy. She was looking at your eyes and she said, "How wonderful it is to see his beautiful eyes peering back at me."

He continued, "As I approached you both, I looked into your eyes and started to cry. Your mother and I were elated with joy to bring you into this world. You brought us both so much happiness. Neither one of us had expected that it was possible to be any happier than we had been."

You were barely two years old when your mother and I were elated to find that she was again with child," continued Alexander.

"I was older than that when Marcus was born," said Alex. He was sure that his father had confused a date.

"True. Marcus was born a few years later. The child that was to be born after you didn't survive. It was very traumatic for your mother. After that, she was never the same again. She blamed me for our loss. The joyful nature of our union began to falter," said Alexander.

"Why did you not tell this to me before?" said Alex.

"I swore to your mother that I would never burden you with this. She always remembered how much joy you brought into her life. It was because of you that she was able to continue with her life. She loved you that much. I am breaking my oath to your mother by revealing this to you. I'm sorry," said Alexander.

"Father, I'm very grateful that you've told me this. But what has this to do with my mother's death," said Alex.

"The doctor had warned us that your mother was not to have any more children, else she might die. As you know, we were blessed with your brother and sister. Each birth was difficult for her, but each brought us both much joy. Although I feared that each birth might further damage her frail body," Alexander said with a glisten of moisture forming in the corner of his eyes. He reached over to the curtain and moved it aside. He peered out the window and slowly started to regain his composure.

Alex moved uneasily in his seat. He was not quite sure how to respond. He felt a little dizzy as he felt a shift begin to ripple through his thoughts. Questions flooded through his head with answers quickly falling into place. Until one question began to form: "Why then was Mother so angry with you all of the time?"

Alexander turned back to Alex.

"As I said before, your mother was very frail. I wanted her to take better care of herself. We often argued about this. As I pushed her to take care of herself, she withdrew farther away. I guess in a way, I did drive her away. I never realized this before. I truly loved her with all of my heart. I could never find a way to draw her back to me..." Alexander tried to continue talking but could not. He tried to speak the words, but nothing came out. He reached for his throat and began to gasp for air.

"Father!" yelled Alex.

A startled Charles and Victoria watched with concern but remained silent as Alex grabbed his father's shoulders and shook him hard.

Alexander's choking episode seemed to subside.

"Father, are you okay?" said Alex.

Alexander heard the concern in his son's voice. It was like a beacon calling him back. He slowly began to speak, "I'm sorry. I have never talked about this to anyone before. I loved your mother very much."

"Thank you for telling me this, Father. I've always blamed you for Mother's death, and now I can see things differently. I was always very close to Mother. She and I would have long talks about what our dreams and ambitions were. She told me about how she had always dreamt about meeting you before you even met. She said that she would tease you and try your patience when you were courting her. She said that she had loved you deeply. I asked her once, why she didn't like you anymore, she got very upset. She said, "I have always loved your father, and I will always love him; just as I have always loved my children."

"I love you very much, Son. As you can see, Mr. and Mrs. Adams have dozed off. Why don't we try to do the same for a little bit? We can talk some more in a little while," said Alexander.

"That's a good idea," said Alex.

Alexander leaned back and closed his eyes.

Alex reached to the curtain and looked outside. After a few minutes, he leaned up against the side of the coach, closed his eyes, and did his best to make himself comfortable. The inside of the coach was not comfortable, but he succumbed to the rhythmic movement of the coach and dozed off. He dreamt about his mother.

Alexander opened his eyes, looked over at his son and felt a wave of pride wash over him. He pulled his hat over his face and began to dream about his wife.

25

The stagecoach driver was feeling restless. He'd made this drive many times, but something was different about today. The air was crisp and fresh. The sky was clear and the sun was bright. Even the horses seemed to be a little off center. They usually looked straight ahead, but they appeared to be distracted by something up in the hills. Even so, they responded very nicely to his words of encouragement. He always enjoyed talking to the horses. He felt that they understood him. Most people thought of him as a very rough and gruff sort of person. But not the horses. They knew that he was a very softhearted person.

Before each trip, the stagecoach driver would show up at the station an hour or so early. He had a routine that he always followed. He would walk over to the stagecoach and inspect every portion of the coach. Then he would walk to the very front of the horses and have a frank conversation with each one. He would speak very softly to each so that no one else would hear him. As he was talking, he would offer each an apple slice. He would always bring a sack of apples from his apple tree just for the trip. He'd pull out his knife, the one that his father gave him. He would slice up the apples one at a time. He loved horses, driving coaches, and the freedom that came from being on the trails far from the city-life.

The coach driver brought his attention back to the road again. He'd been along this path many times before. Weed and brush grew here and there along the road. As roads went, this one was relatively smooth. An occasional misplaced rock would cause a shudder to ripple through the coach, as the wheel collided with it. He thought about the construction of the coach. He thought about how it could absorb some of the bumps and holes that the wheels of the coach had to negotiate. He remembered what the coaches were like just a few short years ago. Now the trains would soon replace the need for the stagecoaches. He was not worried about it. He figured that he had lived a very long, happy, and contented life. How exciting to live in an era of so much change, he thought. He felt a smile starting to form on his face when all of a sudden he saw something moving very high on the side of the mountain. The road that he was traveling on was very narrow but easily maneuverable. To his left was a deep ravine and to his right was the smooth upward slope of the mountain. There were many trees both to his left and to his right that could easily conceal anyone that might want to do so, he thought. He was still feeling uneasy as he sat upright and squinted to see what the movement had been. It could have been a bear, he thought. He'd never seen a bear before, but other coachmen had seen bears roaming in and out of these roads before. He was half way through the narrow trail when all of a sudden a thunderous explosion reverberated through the canyon and startled the horses. The coach veered just enough to the right to graze a rocky outcrop hard that was jutting out from the side of the hill. They stopped so abruptly that the momentum of the coach lunged forward into the horses. The coach driver nearly fell down from his perch and quickly calmed the nervous horses. He could hear a lone scream from the coach as well as grunts and groans from the rest of the passengers. He yelled down into the cabin, "Is everyone all right?"

Alexander answered first, "Yes, what has happened?"

"The thunder has startled the horses. Why don't you all get out for a few moments to stretch your legs? I need to check on the harnesses. Please stay near to the coach," said the coach driver.

Alexander exited the coach first, followed by Mr. and Mrs. Adams and then Alex. Alexander looked up at the sky, it was cloudless.

The red sandy road was rock hard. The silence was deafening.

Charles walked around to the front of the coach to help with the horses. He was talking to them and stroking them on the side of their face. "Everything is okay boys," he said to the horses.

"My goodness, all of this dust! Charles! Charles! Please come over here," Victoria said impatiently.

"Yes, Victoria," Charles yelled.

"Charles!" exclaimed Victoria once more.

Charles patted the horses as he walked over to where his wife was.

"Charles, where did you go?" she said nervously.

"I was just helping our driver calm the horses. They are beautiful beasts. Don't you think?" Charles said. He knew she was a bit nervous standing outside of the safety of the coach. He thought that she would feel safe enough with Mr. Johnson and his son.

Victoria was stern as she spoke, "Charles, It's dangerous out here. Please stay nearby. There could be wild animals out here."

Her demeanor softened, and her eyes darkened.

"Charles, I have a bad feeling about this. I can see that this is a beautiful day. I should not have a worry in the world. But I cannot deny this feeling that I have," she said as her voice trailed off.

Alex was standing next to her.

"Mrs. Adams, please don't worry. Three men here will protect you. We are safe now," Alex said.

Victoria turned to face Alex head on. He looked into her eyes and saw them darken into an ominous frightening shade of midnight.

"Son, you are a gentleman. Your wisdom flows naturally from you," she said and got quiet for a moment. Alex felt uneasy and shot a glance over to his father. He didn't know what to do and then she started to speak very slowly. "Son, please relish each day as if it were your last. You are a person of great conviction. Your father loves you very much and is so happy that you have agreed to meet him again. I'm sorry that the first time did not go as well as you expected, but remember that the bond between you and your father is greater than time itself. You are forming another bond now also. The bond will be one that will help you to grow beyond your expectations. This new relationship will show you the limitation that permeates your existence. You are such a great being who has barely begun to live and grow. I'm sorry for this interruption in your journey. You will complete the journey in a short little while. You will find your father and then your true love again. Just stay the course and let things be as they are. You'll learn that things unfold in ways that support you. Open your mind and let life unfold. You are a great, great being..."

Victoria's knees buckled. She closed her eyes and started to fall.

"Victoria!" exclaimed Charles.

Charles rushed in and caught his wife. Victoria looked up into Charles' eyes.

"What happened?" said Victoria.

She was in her husband's arms.

"Victoria, are you okay? You fainted!" said Charles.

"Yes, of course," she said. She was embarrassed.

"Mrs. Adams, you were speaking quite oddly to me before you fainted," said Alex.

"Oh dear! Charles, please help me into the coach, I'd like to rest for a moment," Victoria said rather nervously.

Charles helped her into the coach and then returned to Alexander and his son.

Alexander asked, "Is Victoria all right?"

"Yes, she's fine. Occasionally she starts to talk strangely. She speaks with the confidence of a great orator and relays wisdom beyond her abilities. When she is in this state, she seems to have an answer for everything. She has never before exhibited this behavior in public. It has always been at home where she is safely seated in her favorite chair," said Charles.

The driver came from around the corner and said, "It's time to go! We have to go back to town, The coach needs a new axle. This one should last us long enough until we get back to town," he said as he pointed to the bottom of the coach. "The coach can leave the hotel early tomorrow morning. I'll be there at 7:00 AM."

No one said a word. The passengers felt uneasy as they boarded the coach. The coach still had a hint of musty atmosphere about it. The cramped quarters held the character of three men and a woman confined on a long dusty trip. As the coach headed back to town, all of them slept, except for Alexander. He just sat there and thought about how close he'd been to reuniting his family.

The stagecoach pulled up to the hotel at 4:00 PM just a half hour after unloading its precious cargo at the local bank.

As the coach was pulling away, Alex said to his father, "Father, I cannot stay here tonight. I'll come back in the morning."

"Son, let's have some dinner before you head back," Alexander said with an air of resignation.

"That sounds like a great idea. I just want to get home before it gets too dark," Alex said.

They had a nice dinner together after which Alexander went back to the hotel and Alex rode home.

Alex was anxious to get home and get a few more things. He'd decided to visit with his family for a little longer. He'd had such a good chat with his father that day, and was so happy that he would soon see Greta, Marissa, and Marcus.

26

When Alex got home, he noticed that Tom's horse was in front. Alex got down from his horse and tied his horse near the water trough. As Alex neared the backyard, he could hear the sheriff and Tom arguing about something interspersed with gunshots. He figured that they were target practicing. He was nearly to the backyard. He could hear very clearly what they were saying. It didn't sound good.

"Uncle, I can't do that to Alex, he's my friend," said Tom.

"Tom, Alex doesn't give a damn about his father, he told me so over and over again. Besides, that stagecoach is carrying a lot of money. It is supposed to leave tomorrow morning for San Francisco at 7:00 AM. I'll make sure that it leaves a little late, about 7:30 to give us some time to get up to the ridge ahead of it. That coach will be in the middle of nowhere, and that's the perfect place to ambush it," said the sheriff

"But…"

"But, nothing. We've done this kind of thing before. Just shut up and make sure that you're at the jail house at half past six tomorrow morning," said the sheriff.

Alex couldn't decide if he should run to warn his father, or stay and reason with the sheriff. The sheriff had always been good to him, he thought. He waited a few more minutes and then he came around the corner of the house.

"Sheriff," Alex called out.

"Alex, what are you doing here?" said Tom with hesitation in his voice.

Neither Tom nor the sheriff suspected that Alex might have heard any of their conversation.

"The stagecoach has a broken axle. We had to come back to get it fixed," Alex said while looking at the sheriff. "I've decided to go visit my family in San Francisco for the next week or so."

"Son, what has gotten into you?" the sheriff said to Alex. The sheriff could not easily conceal his rage. "Your father threw you out of your own home all those years ago, and somehow he's convinced you to go back?"

"I'd like to give him another chance. I'll be joining my father on the coach leaving for San Francisco at 7:30 tomorrow morning," said Alex.

"The coach leaves at 7:00 tomorrow morning," said the sheriff.

The sheriff could always tell when Alex was hiding something.

"You heard us talking about the coach, didn't you?" said the sheriff.

Alex flinched. He'd been caught.

"Sheriff, please leave that coach alone or I'll..." Alex said as he motioned with his hands towards the sheriff.

"Son, are you threatening me?" asked the sheriff.

"No sir, I just..." Alex said as he put his hands down at his side.

The sheriff was enraged. He pulled out his gun and shot at Alex.

Tom screamed, "Why'd you do that?"

"Didn't you see he was reaching for his gun?"

Alex was lying on the ground holding his left arm, writhing in pain. He was not sure what had happened. He was in shock.

"Take care of this mess," said the sheriff.

"He needs a doctor real bad!" Tom said.

The sheriff came back, pointed his gun at Alex's head and fired. Death was instantaneous for Alex.

"Take care of this mess, I said! And don't forget to be at the jail house by half past six tomorrow morning," said the sheriff.

Tom always obeyed the sheriff. He took Alex's limp body to the canyon a few miles from the sheriff's ranch. It was hard for him since

Alex was his only real friend. He never trusted any of his other so-called friends. They'd shoot a bullet through his head if it suited them. Alex was different. He was smart and considerate. He always treated Tom with respect and admiration. He knew that Alex was grateful to him for teaching him how to shoot and ride.

He gave Alex a proper burial. He knew that his uncle would have preferred that he throw him into the ravine to let the coyotes or the mountain lions tear him apart. Instead, Tom dug a grave and carefully placed his friend's body inside. He filled up the void with dirt and put a plain cross where a tombstone would go. He didn't know how to pray, so he just said a few words for Alex to rest in peace, and for the first time in his life, he cried.

Tom got home after dark, cleaned up, and went to bed. He was going to have a very busy day the next day, he thought. He just lay in bed thinking about Alex. He never did fall asleep. In the morning he got up and walked through the house looking for the sheriff. He was gone.

The sheriff was at the bank when the coach arrived the next morning. He told the driver that he had told Mr. Alexander Johnson that he would personally ensure that the cargo from the bank would be loaded onto the stagecoach without incident. This was not true. The sheriff was carefully watching exactly what was loaded onto the coach. There were bank notes, gold, and an assortment of bank documents. The sheriff kept on stopping the clerk each time that the clerk came out of the bank carrying a bag. The clerk was annoyed with the constant interruption, but he would say, "These are bank notes…" or "These are important documents…" or after a while, he would say, "I don't know sir…"

The sheriff noticed that it took two clerks to load two wooden boxes. The clerks very carefully placed these boxes in the coach.

"Gold!" he thought to himself. The sheriff was carefully calculating the value of this bank cargo. Just as the last of the cargo from the bank was loaded, Tom rode up.

"Where have you been? I told you to be here at 6:30," said the sheriff.

"I'm here now," Tom said.

Tom had thought about fleeing back to San Francisco instead of heading into town. He couldn't face Alex's father. Alex had been a very good friend to him and had always looked out for him.

"The coach still has to pick up its passengers. It is running late as it is. Let's get going," said the sheriff.

They both rode off to the north side of town. They traveled along the route that the stagecoach would take. They had been riding for about half an hour when they reached a canyon that had quite a few hiding places. It was not far from the place that Tom had buried his friend. They made their way up a narrow trail to a clearing from which they could see the path below. Large rocks concealed the hiding place from the road. It was just what the sheriff wanted. The sheriff and Tom hardly said a word to each other while they waited. Tom wasn't feeling well. He was still thinking about Alex. Tom saw that his uncle was wide-eyed and barely blinking. He had a crazed look on his face – one of focused determination.

Alexander was almost alone in the town square waiting for the stagecoach as he paced back and forth in the middle of the reddish brown hard clay road. He pulled out his gold pocket watch while he was still pacing on the dusty road. He knew that the stagecoach would have to stop at the bank to load some cargo before picking him up. The coach should have already arrived, he thought. What anyone, even his son, could find comfortable about this small town in the middle of nowhere, he thought. Where is he? The waiting was unbearable – still no coach. He walked over to the hotel porch as the horses, carts, and people began to hustle and bustle about. Alexander was lost in thought, impatient and distracted. At half past eight, the stagecoach arrived in front of the hotel. Alexander snapped out of his distraction in time to see the driver motioning him to enter the coach. The coach was over an hour late, he thought to himself. He took one last look up and down the street and hesitated before entering the coach. If his son were coming, he would have been here already. Was this all for naught, he wondered. Alexander was devastated.

Alexander entered the coach and saw Charles and Victoria Adams seated on the bench nearest to the driver. Victoria noticed that Alexander looked a bit pale and asked, "Mr. Johnson, are you alright? Where is Alex?"

He was devastated. He had been sure that his son was coming back home with him. Alexander had told him that it was his choice. His son looked thrilled at the prospect of seeing his siblings and Gertrude. Perhaps he'd changed his mind when he went back to the sheriff's house. It didn't make sense to him.

"I'm just a little tired," he said with resignation. "He's decided to stay."

Alexander leaned up against the side of the coach, pulled his hat over his face and shut his eyes. He felt defeated and just wanted to go home.

Victoria shot a nervous glance over to her husband. She knew that something was terribly wrong. With that, the coach drove on.

Up on the hill, the sheriff jumped to his feet.

"Get up, boy. They're coming. Get over there and get ready to ride," said the sheriff.

As the coach came around the bend, the sheriff took aim. It was a tricky road for a stagecoach to maneuver through. The road was barely wide enough for the horses and the coach. One side of the road was a deep ravine, which was not too difficult to walk or ride down, but impossible to manage with a stagecoach. Stagecoaches rarely had any trouble in this area as long as they went slowly. The sheriff, an excellent gunman, took careful aim. He paused for a few seconds and then pulled the trigger. The blast reverberated throughout the canyon. The shot hit the driver. The impact threw him off the coach and into the ravine. He died instantly. The horses were startled and the two on the side of the ravine lost their footing and dragged the other horses down the canyon. The coach veered off the road and began to tumble down the canyon wall. The occupants bounced against the inside of the cabin. Alexander fell out of the coach as it began its downward trek.

The coach came to rest near the bottom of the canyon. Luggage, clothing, and papers from the coach were scattered everywhere.

"Tom, I'll head down to the coach and retrieve the cargo. You wait here."

"Yes, sir," said Tom.

The sheriff rode down a small trail that led to the bottom of the canyon. He dismounted from his horse and inspected the coach. He noticed that the two heavy boxes were lying next to the coach. He approached the cabin entrance and heard a scream. Inside he saw a man and a woman, still alive.

"Help us! My husband is barely breathing," said the woman.

The sheriff stepped a little closer and pointed his pistol at the woman's head. The woman was in a darkened cabin looking out at a figure standing in the sun. As the sheriff leaned forward, his shadow crept over her face. She screamed as she recognized the sheriff pointing a gun at her. The sheriff pulled the trigger and then shot again at the husband. They both died instantly.

"Where is Alexander?" muttered the sheriff.

No matter, he thought. He dragged each of the boxes over to a small impression near the crash site. The small impression made an excellent hiding place. He decided to leave the bank notes and other bank papers. He got back on his horse and rode back up to the road where Tom was waiting. The sheriff saw that Alexander was unconscious on the side of the road, and Tom was getting down from his horse.

"What's going on?" said the sheriff.

"He just crawled up here and passed out," said Tom.

The sheriff thought for a minute.

"Get him up on your horse. Let's take him into town," said the sheriff.

The sheriff got off his horse and helped get Alexander's limp body onto the back of Tom's horse.

They rode back into town and dragged Alexander into a jail cell.

"Tom, go get Doc to check him out. Don't say anything, except that you found him wandering out by the canyon. I'll be back later," said the sheriff.

The sheriff went back to the location of the downed stagecoach. He used his horse to pull the boxes on a makeshift cart. He dragged the boxes up to the main road. He just needed to move the boxes just a few hundred feet back towards town to one of his secret hiding places. Only he knew of this location. In this secret hiding place, he had mostly gold and other valuables that he had collected throughout the years. He never told anyone, not even Tom, about his hidden treasures. The secret places were near the major roads leading out of the town. He went back to the stagecoach and sat there for a while. Some of the townspeople were approaching from the town. The sheriff hesitated for a moment. He looked at the stagecoach one last time and then a smile came across his face.

"Sheriff, we're here to collect the cargo," said one of the bank clerks.

The sheriff recognized the bank clerk as the one loading the coach that morning.

"There are three dead bodies here, and the debris is spread out all over here," said the sheriff.

The clerks began to collect the bags with the bank notes and other bank documents.

"We need to right the coach. We can't get to the bank boxes," said one of the clerks.

The other riders, including the sheriff, helped to right the coach. They pulled the two bodies from the coach and placed them respectfully a short distance away.

"The boxes are gone!" exclaimed one of the clerks.

They searched the area and couldn't find any trace of the boxes.

They took the bodies back to the town. The sheriff had convinced them that the lone survivor might be able to tell them what happened to the boxes.

When the sheriff got back to the jailhouse, Alexander was still unconscious.

"Tom, what did Doc say?" asked the sheriff.

"Doc said to just let him sleep it off. He put a splint on his broken leg, but other than that he's going to be fine."

"Was Mr. Johnson drunk?" said the sheriff.

"No. He woke up while Doc was working on his leg. Doc gave him a couple of shots of whiskey to help him with the pain," said Tom.

"Leave him be. Let's go home. I'll come back in the morning to check on him," said the sheriff.

The sheriff checked the cell to make sure that it was secure. He shot a glance at the sleeping Alexander and then smirked. "You botched this stagecoach robbery, you poor bastard."

27

Alexander woke up in the early morning. The sheriff was there.

"Sheriff, what happened? Where am I?" asked Alexander.

"You're in jail, son. Don't you remember?" said the sheriff. "The judge will be back in town tomorrow morning. You'll be tried then."

"Tried? For what? What happened to the coach?" asked Alexander.

Alexander was beginning to remember a little, but he was still confused. He couldn't grasp what was happening to him. The last thing that he remembered was that he was on his way back home and then something happened with the coach, there was an accident.

"Son, what did you do with the gold? Did you think you could get away with this?" said the sheriff mocking him.

"What gold?" Alexander knew that there were bank notes in the coach, but he was not aware of any gold on the coach. He was aware that the bank would often transport gold from the local miners, but he'd been told the day before that there was no gold shipment.

"There were two boxes of gold on that stagecoach. Perhaps if you tell me what you did with those boxes, the judge might take pity on you," the sheriff paused as he looked down at Alexander.

Alexander looked puzzled. Perhaps the bank had decided to add the cargo after he had spoken with them, Alexander thought.

"I've got to go. Someone will be by in a little while with some food," said the sheriff.

"But-"

The door slammed behind the sheriff as he left the jail. Alexander sat back down on the bed and put his head in his hands. He thought that this was some kind of mistake. An error that could easily be fixed, he just didn't know how. Then he thought about his son, Alex. Yes, Alex knew the sheriff. Perhaps if he could just speak with Alex, he could help clear up this mess with the sheriff. The front door opened and in walked Tom with some food and water.

"Sir, here is some food. The sheriff asked me to bring this to you," said Tom.

Tom placed the food in the cell.

"Thank you. Have you seen my son Alex?" said Alexander.

"I haven't seen him today," Tom said nervously. "I have to go. I'll bring some lunch for you around noon."

"If you see him, please ask him to come see me," said Alexander.

Tom looked at Alexander. Tom's eye's widened, his teeth clenched and then turned away.

"Sure," said Tom.

Tom ran out of the building as if there were a fire right behind him. He got on his horse and rode out of town as fast as he could. He couldn't bear to stay in the town any longer. He stopped just outside of town near the canyon where the stagecoach had crashed. He rode up the narrow trail to the small mound where he had buried Alex. He fell to his knees and cried, "Please forgive me, Alex." After a little while, Tom went on his way back to his home in San Francisco.

It was half past noon; the sheriff brought Alexander his lunch. He seemed agitated. "Here's your damn lunch!"

Alexander looked up at the sheriff.

"Where's Tom? He said that he was coming back," said Alexander.

"How in the hell would I know? He's probably causing trouble somewhere. He'll show up. And, when he does, I'll strike the fear of God in him. Now eat your damn food, you son of a bitch!"

"Sheriff, I'm innocent. I didn't steal any gold. I didn't even know there was any gold on the stagecoach. I'm not guilty of anything," said

Alexander.

"Oh, you're guilty all right."

"No, ask my son, he'll tell you."

"Your son said that you asked him to go back with you on that stagecoach. He was laughing his head off when he said that. He told me that you are one crazy old fool that doesn't know how to let go. He said that he'd like to see you rot in jail, or better yet hang."

Alexander was speechless. This didn't make sense. Alex seemed excited to be going home to see his brother, sister, and Gertrude. Something is not right, he thought. He fell back in his bed as he came to the realization that maybe he had been mistaken about his son.

"No, it can't be!" he screamed.

The sheriff was gone as quickly as he had come. Alexander was alone in the dank cell. He looked at his lunch, closed his eyes and then doubled up on his self and threw up.

Alexander fell asleep and hadn't noticed that someone had come in and cleaned up the mess in his jail cell. He woke up. It was dark inside the jail, except for a lamp burning in the far corner of the cell. He saw someone there, but he couldn't quite make out who it was.

"Alex?" Alexander said.

"Just me," said the sheriff. "What the hell happened in your cell? I had to get someone in here to clean up your damn mess."

"I didn't feel too good. Where's my son?"

"Didn't we already talk about this? Now, the judge will be here in the morning. If you just tell me where you hid the gold, I'm sure it'll go easier on you," said the sheriff with a snarl.

"I don't know anything about any gold," said Alexander.

"Well, I thought I'd give you another chance. I reckon that you'll be hanged the day after tomorrow. Hell, if the judge gets here early enough then maybe even tomorrow. I'm going home."

The sheriff snuffed out the lamp and left Alexander sitting alone in his cell. He propped himself up so he could look out the cell window. He held onto the bars with all of his might and screamed, "Something is not right here! I'm not guilty of anything!"

The sheriff turned around and burst out into sinister devilish laughter, "Oh, yes you are!"

Tom was just a few minutes from Marcus's home in San Francisco. He was not sure what he was going to say to Alex's family, but he knew that he had to do this for Alex. He rode up to Marcus's house and saw Marcus in the front yard.

"Marcus!" Tom yelled.

"Tom!" Marcus said excitedly. "Did you talk to Alex? Is he coming?"

"No, he's not coming." Tom got down from his horse and walked over to join Marcus in his front yard.

"I have some terrible news. Your father is in jail for robbing a stagecoach," he said. "The sheriff has gone crazy. Your father didn't rob the stagecoach and your brother…"

"What's this?" Greta asked. She was on the porch and had heard everything.

Tom started to tell them all about what had happened with the stagecoach and that Alexander was in jail. He was talking so fast, he was barely taking a breath as he continued.

"Now slow down. Tell me exactly what happened. Start at the beginning," said Gertrude.

Tom repeated the whole story. He even told her that he had helped the sheriff rob the stagecoach.

"But no one was supposed to be killed. There is one more thing. Like I said, my uncle has gone crazy. He shot Alex. My best friend is dead," Tom looked at Gertrude and then to Marcus. "I'm sorry, I'm sorry," Tom got choked up and couldn't speak.

Marcus fell back in horror, "What?" He was in shock.

"Okay, son, let's go see someone who can help us. Marcus, pull yourself together and take care of your sister. It'll be alright," Gertrude said.

Marcus walked back onto the porch. Marissa was crying. She was saying, "No it won't! No! It won't!"

Gertrude disappeared into the house then made her way to the barn. Within minutes, she came back riding a horse. "Let's go, Tom."

They rode to the bank and found the bank owner. Tom told him the whole story. Of course, the bank owner was in disbelief. Alexander was an exemplary bank manager; he would never resort to such criminal behavior. The bank owner was very familiar with the local law and insisted that they take immediate action. The sheriff was not due to return until late that night. It would be too late to leave that day so they would leave first thing in the morning.

28

The next morning came crawling in like a cat stalking its prey. The sheriff came strolling in with a tray full of food.

"Well, we're in luck. The judge will be here just in time for lunch. It looks like we might have a hanging today after all. Better eat now," said the sheriff.

Alexander picked up his cup and flung it through the bars at the sheriff. It hit the sheriff on the back of the head. Alexander could see that the sheriff was a little too quick to accuse him of this crime. Perhaps the sheriff had robbed the stagecoach himself, he thought.

The sheriff turned around and drew his gun. "You son of a bitch, I should kill you right now!"

The sheriff's eyes were bulging. He was full of rage. There was a barely perceptible shaking in his shooting hand.

Alexander faced the sheriff head on and limped towards the edge of the cell nearest to the sheriff. "Go ahead, shoot. You lying bastard."

The sheriff uncocked his gun and re-holstered it. He burst out laughing again. "Son, you're not as stupid as you look." The sheriff left, still laughing. Alexander looked out the cell window and saw the sheriff shaking his head, as he walked across the way.

"You'll never get away with this, you bastard!" yelled Alexander.

Alexander fell back and sat on the edge of his bed.

"Alex, please forgive me! Please!" said Alexander.

Suddenly he heard a noise come from the other side of the jail.

"Who is there?" he yelled.

There was no response. He peeked around the edge of his cell. This was a vantage point from where he could see the rest of the jail. There was no one there. It was just his imagination. This place is getting to me, he thought.

Four men arrived at the jail right around noon. They escorted Alexander to a building across the way and into the side entrance. He saw several people sitting. A man seated at the table near the front of the room was talking to the sheriff. Alexander tried to speak. Each time he tried, the judge would glare at Alexander with contempt. Time seemed to speed up. Within minutes, the judge found Alexander guilty of murder.

"You are to be hanged," said the judge.

Alexander began to scream, "I'm innocent! What's going on? I'm innocent!"

"Settle down," said the judge while pointing to Alexander. "Escort that man back to his seat!"

Alexander sat down.

"Your honor I request that we do the hanging this afternoon," said the sheriff.

"Granted," said the judge. "Now I have to get back on the road."

The judge stood up and glared at Alexander. Alexander sat dumbfounded.

"Get up," one of the men said.

Alexander, surrounded by four men, limped back to his jail cell; there he would wait. He laid back in his bed and fell asleep. He dreamt about his son Alex. In the dream, Alex was telling him that he forgave him. Alex said that he loved him and that he would help him. Alex also asked him to forgive him for running away. He said that he had always missed him and always loved him.

"Get up you sorry son of a bitch!" yelled the sheriff.

Alexander woke up with a jolt. Three men surrounded him. The sheriff was standing in front.

"Let's go for a walk," said the sheriff still laughing.

Two men picked Alexander up and dragged him down a dark seemingly endless corridor. The third man was walking just behind him muttering a prayer of sorts: "Though I walk through the shadow of the valley of death..." His adrenaline was pumping while his breathing became shallow and erratic. Beads of sweat, forming under his brow, flowed relentlessly into his eyes. The corridor led out back to an open area. There in the center of the open area was a wooden structure with stairs leading up to a platform. There was a rope hanging from a structure in the center of the stage. It took a couple of minutes for Alexander to realize what the structure really was. He had never seen gallows before. Alexander was limping. Two men were holding him as he hobbled his way up to the structure. The sheriff was walking behind Alexander.

"Please let me see my son," Alexander said with an air of resignation.

The three of them made their way up the stairs and were nearly to the hanging rope, when the sheriff leaned over and whispered into Alexander's ear, "I shot him in the head. The fool was going to go back with you. Now you can go join that son of a bitch in hell."

The others did not hear those icy words that stabbed at Alexander's heart. His eyes widened with shock as his body tensed with rage. The sheriff was laughing. The sheriff stopped laughing when he saw Alexander suddenly stop and turn. The two men escorting Alexander fumbled as Alexander lunged at the sheriff knocking him down. Alexander pummeled the sheriff who was lying on his back completely overwhelmed. The other two men recovered quickly and pulled Alexander up and off the sheriff. The red-faced sheriff jumped to his feet and planted his tightly clenched fist squarely on Alexander's nose. Blood began to flow down Alexander's broken nose. The sheriff grabbed the hood that would have covered Alexander's head for the hanging. He wiped his bloody hand on it and tossed it to the ground below. The other two men dragged him over to the center of the platform. There before him, Alexander saw the noose. The realization of what was about to happen hit him like a ton of bricks. He muttered, "Why?" They shoved him forward. He did not resist.

"Hang that son of a bitch! He's crazy! He tried to kill me! Hang him!" yelled the sheriff.

Alexander felt the cold, stiff rope fit tightly around his neck. The rope had a wet dank smell. He was giving up. He had failed. The door below his feet gave way. He felt weightless for an instant followed by a large cracking noise. He tried to gasp for air to no avail. His eyes bulged open. He could see crowds of people watching him, gawking at him. He saw images in his head. He saw images of his family, images of his life, and images of his failures. He tried breathing. He tried gasping for air and then all of a sudden his body stopped trying. His neck hurt. He felt cold.

Alexander hung from a rope with a noose tightly wrapped around his neck. His eyes were bulging from his head, and they were still imprinting images onto his retina from the direction that his head was facing. The tension on the rope was enormous. Each of the strands of the rope buckled as the pressure caused them to pull apart. As they pulled apart, the rope twisted in a cruel and morbid circular rotation. Alexander's body started to turn to his right ever so slowly.

His mouth tried in vain to speak the words, "Alex, I love you. I'm so sorry." Of course, there was no air to make any sound. Just then, something caught his eye off to his left. His pupils became pinpoint sharp as his body turned straight on to see a half dozen men approaching on horseback. He recognized his younger son, the bank owner, and others. He thought that the cavalry was coming to save him. His thinking was erratic. One moment he was in a coach with his eldest son going home, and now this moment he was watching his youngest son fast approaching. As his body continued to turn, he saw the sheriff riding towards the approaching horsemen. "The light of the sun was gone," he thought. He turned once again and saw the sheriff drawing his gun toward the approaching riders.

"No!" he wanted to say. He heard several booming gunshots. He thought that he felt the percussion of weapons fire on his entire body.

His eyes locked straight ahead of his nearly lifeless body and continued to record the agonizing sights. His eyes were bulging yet still registering images. He wanted to smile as he saw the sheriff fall to the ground dead. He couldn't breathe. He had lost his son, his family and his life. He had lost it all. The darkness in his eyes grew as his pupils dilated. The darkness filled him completely. Then he saw nothingness. He felt nothingness. This was more than he could bear. He could hear a snap like crashing thunder as the rope tightened around his neck. The rope was pulling him upwards. The earth was pulling him downward, both conspiring to rob him of his life. He died.

Alexander found himself at his home. He still felt disoriented; he was just so relieved to be home. He found it odd that everyone was gone. "No matter," he thought. He was exhausted and could only think of finally resting in his own bed. He made his way to his bed and sat down on the edge. He rubbed his sore neck. It occurred to him for just an instant that he might be more comfortable if he removed his traveling clothing. Instead, he laid back and drifted into a deep, dark sleep from which he would not wake for a very long time.

Gertrude was cleaning up the kitchen when she thought she heard the front door. She turned around and for an instant caught a glimpse of Alexander. A feeling of nausea swept through her. With an air of trepidation, she reached for a cloth to dry her hands and called out. "Alexander! What happened? Where is Alex?"

There was no answer.

Gertrude walked briskly to catch up with Alexander. As she turned the corner, there was no one there. She checked Alexander's room and found it undisturbed. As she was closing the door, she saw a stack of papers sitting on the edge of Alexander's desk, and a few lying on the floor. She hadn't noticed these earlier. She walked over to the desk and picked up the papers from the floor. They were letters. She looked at several of them and noticed that each started with "Dear Son…" She realized that Alexander had written these letters to his Alex. She sat down and looked at the stack of papers on the desk. They were letters too. She looked back at the letters in her hand and the one on top.

Son,

   I received your letter asking that I not contact you. It hurts me very much. But I will honor your request. We are all anxious to reunite with you. I love you very much, Son. And I hope that someday you will return and forgive me.

Father

She put the letters back on top of the others and used her handkerchief to wipe away her tears.

She went to the sitting room where Marissa was reading a book.

"Marissa, did you just come in?" said Gertrude.

"No," she replied nervously. "I've been sitting here reading, or at least trying to read this book," Marissa paused for an instant then put her book down. "Gertrude, I just can't get over this horrible feeling. Things are dreadful now, and I feel that everything will be even worse. Neither one of them had wanted to talk about Alex. Perhaps they had hoped that what Tom had told them might not be true somehow.

"I wish that Father had not left. When will Father be back?" Marissa asked.

Gertrude did not answer.

"Gertrude!" Marissa exclaimed. She could see a glaze of concern frost over Gertrude's eyes. This frightened Marissa. She knew instantly what this meant; she felt it in her bones.

"Yes," Gertrude said softly. Gertrude also knew the feeling of dread. She knew that something had gone terribly wrong. She knew that Alexander was dead.

29

Alexander, in a deep slumber since his tragic death in 1864 started to awaken. It was a new time for him. It was 1942. It was an era where oil lamps and stagecoaches were not commonplace; instead, there was electricity and automobiles.

"Come Alexander. It is time to be born again. It is time to complete what you started. It's time," Martha called out. She was calling to Alexander softly and lovingly. Martha was now Carmen, mother of four children of her own. She had married her loving husband, Enrique in 1932. Ten years later, they were living in San Antonio awaiting the birth of their fifth child.

"Carmen, be reasonable. The doctor has said that if you continue with this pregnancy, you will die," Enrique said in spanish to his wife.

"I'm fine. The doctor is wrong. He doesn't care about us. He could not even understand what we were saying. He could barely speak spanish," Carmen said desperately to Enrique.

"We were lucky that he was able to see us. He is very busy!" Enrique said briskly. He was mortified at the thought of losing his wife. She meant everything to him, and he could not bear to live without her. He loved her deeply.

"The doctor is wrong!" she yelled at Enrique as she wiped away her tears.

She went back to the kitchen and finished washing the dishes. It had already been a very long day for her. She put the children to bed and retired to her room. Enrique was already sleeping.

"I love you," she said to her husband who was snoring loudly.

At twenty-eight, she had already given birth to four beautiful children: two boys and two girls. She loved them with all of her heart. She felt that this baby was going to be a special child. She'd been dreaming about the baby for months. As she lay in bed, she felt the cool breeze of the night air flowing through the open window ever so softly. The curtains swayed gently as the air moved towards her and caressed her face. She smiled and placed her hands lightly on her belly.

"It's you, my beautiful child. I love you so much. I can hardly wait for you to come back into this world. I have missed you so much. You will love your new brothers and sisters. They are very excited to welcome you," Carmen said in a delicate whisper to her unborn child.

Another couple of weeks went by after the doctor had recommended the termination of the pregnancy. Carmen had continued to resist the pressure that the doctor, her husband, and his family were exerting on her to give up her unborn child.

She and Enrique were visiting Enrique's parents a few days later.

"This baby must be born!" she said under her breath as she saw her mother-in-law Margarita coming down the stairs to greet her.

"Carmen I'm happy to see you. How are you doing?" Margarita said affectionately to Carmen.

"I'm all right," Carmen said softly. She was usually an outspoken, independent woman, but now she felt wary. Enrique had told her that his mother wanted to talk to her about the baby. Enrique had disappeared into the kitchen. She was alone with her mother-in-law.

"Carmen, you must do the right thing. Enrique is worried about you. You must go to the hospital," Margarita said to Carmen. Margarita was the powerful matriarch of the family. Carmen loved and trusted her mother-in-law and would never think of disobeying Margarita.

"But..." Carmen said so quietly that Margarita didn't hear her.

"We love you very much. We want you to be with us for a very long time. I lost a child too and not a day goes by that I wish that things were different. It still hurts very much," Margarita said to Carmen.

Carmen was shocked. She hadn't known that Margarita had lost a child. She was speechless. Margarita's eyes had become grave and moist with tears. Carmen still wanted to keep her unborn baby, but Margarita's disclosure was so compelling. She felt like she no longer had a choice.

"Okay. If you think that it is the right thing to do," Carmen said.

Margarita leaned in closer to Carmen and then gave her a big hug. They both cried for a long time.

They visited for a little while longer and then went back home. Enrique wasted no time; he made an appointment with the doctor for the next day.

That night Carmen had a restless sleep. She dreamt that she'd been lying in bed as the breeze coming from the window turned violent. It was no longer softly caressing her cheeks, but instead pelting her face with sharp, piercing raindrops. She got up from bed to close the window as the water drenched her while the blasts of lightning illuminated her bedroom. She looked out into the street and saw a man that looked oddly familiar. He was waving to her. She was stunned, and not quite understanding what was happening. She looked over at her sleeping husband and called out to him. "Enrique, come here! There is a man outside."

Enrique didn't wake. She thought it was odd that he was sleeping through this. She shifted her gaze ever so slightly and was shocked to see that her body was still sleeping right next to Enrique.

"It's me," she heard the man yell from outside the window. The man had crossed the street and was standing near the walk that led to the front door. "Please, come to the porch and talk to me. It's important."

Carmen felt a wave of calm wash over her. "Okay, I'll be right there."

She looked over at the bed where she and her husband were sleeping and made her way to the front porch. The rain had stopped and the night air was crisp and refreshing. The man sat on the bench by the front door. Carmen had to walk around him to get to the other side of the bench. She favored the porch swing, but it was still wet. She sat down next to him.

"Do you recognize me? I'm Alexander," he said to Carmen.

Carmen looked up in surprise. She'd thought that she recognized him the moment she saw him standing across the road, but she couldn't quite place him. She looked into the man's eyes. Suddenly memories of love and heartache came to her. She knew who he was.

"Yes! Yes! I remember!" she said with a broad smile planted on her face. "I've missed you. I've been calling to you for a very long time." It was as if her persona changed from Carmen to Martha.

"I heard you. I finally heard you. But why…" Alexander trailed off.

"Why what?" she said.

"Why won't you let me be born? It is my time," he said.

She looked down as she fought to hold back her tears. A single tear had escaped. It was halfway down her cheek when she wiped it away.

"I'm not strong enough. My husband and his mother won't listen to me," Carmen said. "I pray each night that my baby will be born strong and healthy. However, the doctor has said that the baby and I would not survive. I don't believe him, but no one will listen to me. Enrique is scared that I will die. His fear is clouding his judgment. He loves me too much to take a risk that I might die. He thinks that his life would be over if I were to die."

"The darkness that killed our son continues. That darkness cannot again be responsible for my death," the man said with uncertainty in his voice.

Carmen burst into tears as she remembered the loss of Martha's son Alex. She remembered how happy that Alex had been when she came to collect him after his death. Alexander, on the other hand, was writhing in pain and consumed with sorrow and hate when she came for him. As he was hanging from the rope, he thought that he'd glimpsed the image of his wife, but he couldn't hear her.

"Can you not come back just a little later?" she asked.

"Yes, but…" he said as his voice trailed off.

Alexander began to fade from her view and she found herself back in bed.

"But what?" she screamed.

"Carmen, are you okay?" Enrique was sitting up reaching for her hand. "You are drenched. Do you have a fever?" He put his hand on her forehead.

"I'm okay," Carmen said as she was wiping the tears away from her eyes. "I just had a bad dream."

"We have to be at the hospital in two hours. Will you be ready? My mother will watch the children," Enrique said nervously. He had started to think that maybe his wife was right about the doctor. The doctor that they had spoken to was making house calls and a different doctor was going to perform the procedure.

"Yes. I'll be ready," Carmen said hopefully. She saw doubt creeping into her husband's eyes. She hoped that Enrique would change his mind. The choice was in God's hands now, she thought to herself.

"I'll be right back," said Enrique. He went for a short walk to smoke a cigarette and clear his head. When he came back, he'd decided (or rather convinced himself) that it was the right thing and the only thing to do.

Carmen reached for her rosary that she kept under her pillow and said the prayers of the Rosary. It took fifteen minutes for her to recite all of the prayers. She wasn't sure if she missed some of the Hail Marys as she took each of the beads between her thumb and finger. After she was finished, she carefully stowed the rosary under her pillow and took a quick bath.

"Carmen, let's go!" yelled Enrique from the front room. He had his keys in his hands and his wife's bag.

"I'm coming," she yelled back. She had been crying while she was in the bath. She had no more tears to shed. She felt victimized and alone. Others were deciding her destiny. His name is going to be Michael, she thought to herself.

They arrived at the hospital and walked up to the counter full of nurses that only spoke english. Enrique's english was so broken that they could not understand him. It took a few minutes to find a nurse that spoke spanish. She coordinated the admittance and took Carmen to her room.

"Thank you," said Carmen. "You are so kind to help me."

"I'll be right back," the nurse said in spanish. The nurse left as two other nurses helped Carmen into the waiting bed.

Carmen had not noticed that there were other patients in the room until she heard a woman cough a few feet away from behind the curtains to her left. She looked around the room. The room was sterile and smelled of alcohol. She turned her head, planted her face squarely into the pillow, and began to cry. The woman in the next bed turned in the direction of the soft cries that were coming from behind the curtain. She looked down at her own belly as she caressed it with her hand and mourned her loss.

The next day Carmen lay helpless in a brightly lit room. She was barely aware of the doctor and the nurses that were in the room with her.

"This woman is quite a bit further along than I thought," he said as he proceeded to deliver the baby. The nurses looked at each other but said nothing.

The baby's full body was in the doctor's hands. He reached over and turned the baby so that it was face down. He skillfully withdrew the head from the safety of the womb. It was a breach birth. This doctor prided himself in his success record with complicated deliveries. He'd been directed to end the pregnancy as quickly as possible by the woman's doctor, but couldn't help showing off a bit in front of the nurses.

"Doctor, the baby looks healthy," the nurse said smiling with pride to the doctor.

"Nurse, mind your business! Tend to the patient!" he said sternly to the nurse that was assisting him.

"I'm sorry, Doctor," the nurse said as she turned her attention to Carmen.

The baby was nearly full term. It was a boy. The doctor handed the baby to a large nurse who was standing near the far side of the room.

"You know what to do," he said quietly to her. "I'll finish up with the mother."

She took the baby into an adjoining room. The baby was spreading its little arms slowly with considerable strength. She put the baby down on the table and started to wrap the baby with a cloth as the ancient Egyptians would wrap their dead. She started at the feet, binding the fabric so tight that the baby couldn't move. She was surprised at how much the baby was fighting. Perhaps, he was fighting for his life, she thought. He won't survive anyway, she thought. She had done this so many times already, but she never got used to it. She felt justified in saving the mother's life. Although, this baby seemed to be a little older than the others were. These Mexicans have so many babies, she thought.

"Before long, your mother will have another and then another," she said to the baby.

She lifted the baby and held his arms down while she wrapped the cloth tight against his body. The baby was suffocating. The baby was dying. The baby was turning blue as the tightly bound material crushed his chest. One arm had slipped out and was flailing wildly. She lost her grip on the baby. He came crashing down, head first on the hard table. She picked him up and saw that the baby's malleable skull had flattened at the site where it had hit the table. The flailing had stopped. The head was hanging limply. His head was throbbing, as his consciousness was withdrawing. His little heart continued to beat for another minute before he completely passed out. He thought about his wife, Martha and then about his son, Alex. He died. He died before he ever had a chance to live. He had died before he had the opportunity to make things right with his son.

The doctor told Enrique that the baby had died at birth.

After four years of mourning, Carmen had two more daughters. They were there to help Carmen heal. The healing was miraculous. After that, she had four more children who heard her call to be born. One of which was Alexander who heard and answered her call again, this time as Roger who was born in 1955. However, the trauma of the near birth in 1942 haunted Roger for several years and delayed Roger from being present in this life. He suffered from nightmares. In his nightmares, he was suffocating. He felt cloth tightly wrapped around his chest, just like a cocoon. He would eventually wake up choking with a strong metallic taste in his mouth. He would cry incessantly for reasons that his parents never understood. Roger's oldest sister, who called him "Mickey" would often comfort him. Roger didn't understand that he had remembered his death in 1942.

30

In 1958, Roger, a little boy of three years old sat with his toys in the front living room of a modest size house that his parents had bought back in 1945. Carmen, Roger's mother, was busy in the kitchen washing the dishes from the noontime meal. Enrique, Roger's father, had come home from work for lunch and was taking a short nap before heading back to his job as a Life Insurance salesman.

Roger's full attention was on stacking some wooden blocks, one on top of the other until they nearly reached the sky, or so it seemed to him. He would suddenly strike the middle block with his little hand and watch the pieces go flying across the linoleum floor. Each time that Roger knocked over the blocks, he would meticulously gather each of the blocks and reconstruct his tower. One of the blocks made its way under the couch. He reached underneath and felt something small and familiar. It was one of his favorite toys. It felt like the toy that he had lost long ago. He pulled the small plastic figure out from underneath the couch. It was a little cowboy. He smiled at the sight of his favorite little toy. He drew it close to him and examined the detail of the face. It was somehow familiar. His thoughts started to wander as he looked straight into the eyes of the little cowboy. He slowly stood up, reached for his throat and coughed. The memory of a nightmare he sometimes had came fluttering into his mind. In the nightmare, he would find himself gasping for air while holding his throat. He jumped when he heard a loud thunderous noise come from the front yard. If he was a little older, he might have thought that it was a gunshot or a car backfiring. He was only three. The symptoms suddenly disappeared. He walked ever so slowly to the front screen door and opened it just enough to fit his little body through. He squeezed through the opening and carefully made his way to the edge of the concrete stairs. There were so many of them, he thought. There was usually someone around that would insist on helping him descend the stairs safely, but little Roger would prefer to negotiate each step one at a time by himself. He knew that if he got into trouble, then someone would be nearby to catch him if need be. However, this time, he was on his own. He stopped for a moment with his little toes curled over the edge of the top step. He made his way over to the side of the steps so that he could hold on to the wall that framed the concrete stairs. The first step was a little tricky for him, but then the next step seemed easier. He took the rest of the steps one at a time until he reached the bottom. He sat down for a moment on the bottom step and looked out towards the road. He still had his little cowboy in his hand. He'd been careful not to drop it, for if he lost it out here, he would never be able to find it again. He once again drew that small being close to his face and admired the fine detail of his little charge. A smile of remembrance warmed his face. He stood up and walked over to the edge of the road. He looked up and down the street and saw no one else. It was just he and his little plastic cowboy. He started to walk up the road, hoping to find his real life cowboy. Someone yelling from a distance behind him startled him. Little Roger continued walking up the road slowly.

The house was located right next door to a telephone company where Jessie, a man in his thirties, was putting gasoline into the phone company truck. Jessie was a very friendly and dedicated worker who knew the whole family as well as most of the neighbors on the block. He would never miss an opportunity to say hello to anyone passing by. He was never invited over for dinner or anything like that. Even so, Roger's siblings and his parents liked Jessie very much. Jessie noticed

MY LITTLE COWBOY

a little boy crossing the telephone company driveway headed towards busy Ashby Avenue. He noticed that the little boy had turned back a few times and seemed to be looking for someone on the road. The boy continued on his trek toward the busy road. Jessie realized that little Roger was alone on the road. Jessie quickly ran around the truck and saw Mrs. Mendoza through the kitchen window.

"Mrs. Mendoza! Mrs. Mendoza!" yelled Jessie.

Carmen looked up to see Jessie standing near the fence frantically waving his arms at her.

"Your little boy is walking up the road!" Jessie said as he started to run after little Roger.

Carmen quickly shut off the water and did not even bother to dry her hands. She ran to the living room where her little boy had been playing and saw the rubble of small wooden blocks strewn about the floor. Her heart sank, and fear crept deep into her chest. Without thinking, she flung the screen door open, ran down the stairs, and saw her vulnerable little child disappear around the corner of the telephone company building. Jessie was running down the driveway towards the road. Carmen turned the corner in time to see Jessie catch up with him. Roger resisted Jessie's help. Roger pulled away from Jessie and started to run. Jessie was faster and took hold of little Roger's hand.

"Rogelio!" Carmen screamed. The sound of her voice was one of sheer terror.

She ran over to Roger and picked him up. She clutched him close to her as she ran back to the house. "Thank you, Jessie!"

"You're welcome, Mrs. Mendoza. He's okay," said Jessie.

She walked into the living room and locked the screen door behind them. She put Roger down on the couch.

"What were you doing outside, my baby?" she said, her voice quivering. She was both angry and relieved.

"I was looking for my little cowboy," Roger said with a sigh.

Roger's baby brother had started to cry. Barely one year old, Bobby had been napping in the room next to the kitchen. She looked over at Roger's little hand and saw a small toy cowboy.

"Well, there he is!" her voice softening a bit as she spoke. She turned and went off in the direction of the tearful wailing.

"No, Mommy, I didn't find my little cowboy," Roger whispered. He looked over to the front door. "He was supposed to be outside by the road waiting for me so that we could go home. But he wasn't there!"

He looked down at his precious little plastic toy that he was tightly clutching in his right hand. He looked at it once again, and then slowly put his prized possession in his pants pocket. He looked once more towards the front door. "Don't worry, my little cowboy, I will find you. I promise. I love you, Son."

A warm sensation of recognition filled his little heart as his eyes began to well up with tears of joy. The emotion was so overwhelming for this little boy. He almost started to cry, but then he noticed that his favorite blocks were all over the floor. He wiped away his tears as he got down from the couch and walked over to them and collected each one of them. He began to stack them one upon another and then topple them when they were four or five blocks high. His world had returned to normal. He was happy once again.

THE END

ACKNOWLEDGMENTS

I have been inspired to write by everyone that I've ever met. I'm so thankful for all of the experiences - both positive and negative that added so much diversity to my life.

I am so grateful to my friend Gina Hendershot. We have spent many hours talking about my book, reincarnation and many other topics. Thanks so much for the suggestions, the critiques, the editing and the support. This has helped me to gain a deeper understanding of my work, my views, and my ideas. She edited the first edition of this book.

A special thanks to my brothers and sisters. Each has added so much to my life. My parents added everything else.

And thanks to the regression hypnotist, who guided me through a past life regression using hypnosis. I've never done such a thing. The session confirmed my unusual experiences in remembering my past life.

PRINCIPLES

PAST AND PRESENT LIVES

Alexander Johnson- b. 1817; d 1864
    Husband of Martha, Father of Alex, Marcus, and Marissa
    Then born as Michael b. 1942, d. 1942
    Then born as Roger - b. 1955

Martha- b. 1821, d. 1851
    Wife of Alexander Johnson
    Then born as Carmen - b. 1914, d. 1996

Alex - b. 1841, d. 1864
    Son of Alexander Johnson

Marcus - b. 1845, d.1909
    Son of Alexander Johnson

Marissa - b. 1848, d. 1913
    Daughter of Alexander Johnson

Gertrude - b. 1798, d. 1881
    Martha's adopted aunt

Tom - b. 1840, d. unknown
    Alex's best friend

Jane
    Alex's girlfriend

Sheriff Thomas Buchanan - b. 1817, d. 1864
    Brother of Elizabeth

Elizabeth
    Tom's mother

CHRONOLOGY OF EVENTS

1792	Martha's mother is born
1795	John, Martha's uncle (The brother of Martha's mother) is born
1798	Gertrude is born on 11/21/1798
1816	Gertrude's wedding day to John (Greta is 18, John is 21) on 12/20/1816
1817	Sheriff Thomas J. Buchanan Born on 5/17/1817
1817	Alexander Sr. born on 9/6/1817
1821	Martha is born on 11/9/1821
1838	Alexander Sr. Meets Martha on 1/2/1838
1840	Alexander marries Martha on 3/14/1840
1841	Alex, Alexander and Martha's firstborn is born on 9/25/1841
1841	"A Journey to California" guidebook is published
1843	Martha is pregnant with her second child on 2/5/1843
1843	Move from New York to California (six-month trek) on 4/1/1843
1843	Arrive at new home in California (San Francisco) on 10/1/1843
1843	Martha and Alexander lose their baby on 10/24/1843
1843	Martha's baby had been due to arrive on 11/5/1843 (but had died)
1845	Marcus was born on 3/13/1845
1845	"The Emigrants Guide to Oregon and California" guidebook is published
1845	"The Gold Regions of California" is published
1848	Gold is discovered in Coloma, California on 1/24/1848
1848	Marissa is born on 8/22/1848
1850	California becomes a state
1850	Martha becomes very ill on 12/23/1850
1851	Martha dies on 9/25/1851
1857	First interior stagecoach service from Portland, Oregon to Salem, Oregon
1858	The Overland Mail Company ran a tri-weekly stage between San Francisco and Los Angeles using Concord Coach to San Jose and the canvas covered thoroughfare wagons the rest of the distance
1858	Alex Jr. leaves home on 9/25/1858
1858	The Overland Mail Company took 24 days for the first Overland mail from St. Louis, MO to San Francisco. The route was

	published as 2700 miles, but the inaugural trip was actually 2866 miles due to detours
1859	Leavenworth and Pikes Peak Express Stagecoach reach Denver (from Leavenworth to Riley, Kansas into Colorado, Cherry Creek) on 5/1/1859
1859	William H. Russell established the Pony Express. Worked out trail between St. Joseph, Missouri and Sacramento, California. They built stations at ten-mile intervals. Mail delivered within ten days. Sold in 1866 to Wells Fargo
1859	Wells & Fargo expanded operations north into Seattle
1860	The Pony Express makes its inaugural trip on 4/3/1860
1860	The courtship of Alex and Jane begins 9/1860
1860	Two days ride on the stagecoach from Los Angeles to San Diego (Day One Leave San Diego 5 am - Arrive San Juan Capistrano 7:00 PM; Day Two Arrive Los Angeles 4:00 PM. Stagecoaches ran ten to fifteen mph
1863	Alex decides to propose to Jane 9/1863
1864	Alex and Jane planned to marry and move to San Francisco in October
1864	Alex Jr. dies on 9/22/1864
1864	Stagecoach Accident. Alexander lone survivor, stagecoach driver and Mr. and Mrs. Adams are killed on 9/23/1864
1864	Alexander Sr. moves on 9/25/1864
1864	Sheriff Thomas J. Buchanan moves on 9/25/1864
1942	Carmen loses baby (Alexander Sr. from 19th century)
1955	Roger is born (Alexander Sr. from 19th century)
2005	Past life revealed to Roger in an unusual way
2010	Roger visits past life regression hypnotist
2012	The first edition of this book is published
2016	The second edition of this book is published

ABOUT THE AUTHOR

Roger Mendoza lives in San Antonio, Texas, the seventh largest city in the United States. In 2014, he moved back to his birth town of San Antonio from Parker, Colorado where he had lived for fifteen years. Living on the outskirts of San Antonio, he still enjoys the taste of the rural life that he loves so much and the many conveniences that the big city provides.

He worked most of his life as a Software Engineer in the defense industry where he cultivated his passion for computer programming but is now retired. Along with writing novels, Roger is also a professional photographer and can often be seen toting his camera looking for photo opportunities in and around town. He loves to capture nature photography and beautiful scenery.

He was born eighth in a family of ten children. There were five boys and five girls with an age span of about twenty-three years. With a fascination for his family history, he has spent years gathering his parent's family photographs and documents. He has cataloged the family's collections and digitized them all. He loves keeping the family tree database updated with new family members as they are born. Roger loves to review the thousands of family photographs and documents while imagining what these people – these relatives were like.

Roger has always had an interest in understanding the philosophy of life, why people act the way they do and how we all fit into the grander scheme of life itself. He still believes in 'happy endings' even though life often gets in the way of that outcome on occasion.

He's always had a fascination with unusual phenomena – the most being the drama of life itself. It still amazes him why so much drama fills the life of his friends and family. Perhaps it is observing that drama that sparks his imagination and gives his characters life.

BOOK CLUB QUESTIONS

1. Do you believe in past lives and reincarnation? Why or why not?

2. Do you think that Alexander not being born in 1942 messed up Roger's current life?

3. When Roger went back to playing with his blocks at the end of the book, could the author have been suggesting that focusing on the present made Roger happy?

4. Why would Roger's past life reveal itself to him while driving on the freeway? And why was it revealed in two parts?

5. Do you think Tom really thought of Alex as a friend?

6. What is the significance (if any) of the following story elements?
   - Alexander gave Alex some gold nuggets when they reunited.
   - Little Alex playing with blocks as a child and Roger playing with blocks as a child. Did that event combined with finding the little plastic toy cowboy trigger the past life recall?

7. What do you think of Roger's explanation of the 'Thought-Collective' in the Preface?

8. Have you ever met someone that you immediately felt like you'd known all your life?

9. Would you ever participate in a hypnosis session to see if you have a past life?

10. The story suggests that life always finds a way to bliss, even if interrupted. And the author believes in happy endings. Now is there such a thing as: "And they all lived happily ever after?"